# Great
# Michigan
# Deer Tales

# Book 5

# Great Michigan Deer Tales Book 5

## Stories Behind Michigan's Biggest Bucks

### Richard P. Smith

Smith Publications

# Great Michigan Deer Tales - Book 5
## Stories Behind Michigan's Biggest Bucks

## by Richard P. Smith

Published by:
 **Smith Publications**
 Richard P. Smith
 Lucy J. La Faive
 814 Clark St.
 Marquette, MI 49855

Copyright © 2009 by Richard P. Smith
First Printing 2009
Printed in the United States of America

All photos by the author unless otherwise credited
Cover photo by Richard P. Smith
Back cover design plan by Lucy J. La Faive
Cover and Interior Layout by Globe Printing - www.globeprinting.net

**Library of Congress Cataloging in Publication Data**
Smith, Richard P.
Great Michigan Deer Tales - Book 5: Stories Behind Michigan's Biggest Bucks/
by Richard P. Smith
Deer hunting–Michigan
SK 301.S6 2009 bk.5      799.27SM bk.5
ISBN 978-0-9710355-2-2 Softcover

*FOR BRUCE A. SMITH,*
*my brother who I have*
*shared many great deer*
*tales with, with more to come!*

# Contents

# *Acknowledgments*

First and foremost I would like to acknowledge and thank all officers and measurers, past and present, of Commemorative Bucks of Michigan (CBM) for their efforts in measuring many of the big antlered bucks bagged in the state each year and for maintaining a dependable set of records that are becoming an increasingly valuable reference for all big game hunters interested in trying their luck in Michigan. These records help promote the state and give it the credit that's due as a quality whitetail producer. Through the help of CBM, I have been able to locate and interview most of the hunters mentioned in this book.

CBM's records are referred to frequently on the pages that follow to help put the size of the racks that are discussed in perspective. How the antlers rank in the county where they were taken and on a statewide basis is mentioned in most, if not all, cases. However, those rankings can change from year-to-year and those that appear in the chapters of this book were current at the time the book was written.

Hunters do not have to have bagged a buck or any other trophy animal that qualifies for state records to belong to CBM. Annual memberships are $25. To join, send a check or money order to CBM, P.O. Box 2477, Howell, MI 48844. For additional information call 810-796-2925 or 800-298-2925. The toll free number only works in Michigan.

If you have bagged a buck with antlers that might qualify for listing in state records, you should have the rack measured. It doesn't matter what year the deer was killed.

A list of CBM's statewide network of scorers, along with their addresses and telephone numbers, is on CBM's web site: www.buckfax.com. Contact the CBM representative nearest you to make an appointment to have your antlers measured. All racks taken during the current season must air dry for 60 days before they can be officially scored. The deadline for each year's scoring period is March 31. There's a nominal charge to enter antlers in state records that meet minimum qualifications, for hunters who do not belong to the organization. Members can enter as many as they wish at no charge.

I also want to publicly thank all of the deer hunters who have shared their tales with me so I could write about them and allowed me the opportunity to photograph their trophy bucks. Extra appreciation goes out to the hunters who have allowed me to use photographs they have provided of their trophy whitetails. I never tire of hearing exciting deer tales, especially those dealing with big bucks, and seeing the trophy animals. An even bigger thanks goes out to family and friends who I have hunted with, sharing deer tales on another level.

My wife Lucy deserves special credit as my partner who published this book as well as took care of many of the other important details and work required to complete this book. Her skill and foresight have made me more efficient in my writing as well as looking after many important business and personal details so I can concentrate on one of my life's passions - DEER HUNTING!

# *Introduction*

"This is the first time that such detailed coverage of so many of the state's biggest bucks has been presented in book form. I thought it was about time. I hope you agree. If enough of you do, another book including different deer tales may be possible for the future."

Those are the last sentences I wrote for the introduction to the first book of Great Michigan Deer Tales, which was published in 1994 to commemorate the 100th anniversary of licensed deer hunting in the state. Obviously, plenty of deer hunters were interested in a book devoted to detailed stories behind the biggest bucks bagged by hunters in Michigan. That book was so popular, it sold out in a matter of a few months and was reprinted in 1995.

Due to the interest in those stories, and, as promised, a new batch of great deer hunting stories were published in Book 2 during 1998. Interest in Book 1 remained high, resulting in it being reprinted again during 2000. Book 3 came along in 2001, then Book 4 in 2005.

You are now reading Book 5 in the series to meet the continued demand for stories about great deer hunts, great deer and great deer hunters from the great state of Michigan. This book was published to commemorate the 115th anniversary of licensed deer hunting in the state and the grand traditions that have evolved around this cherished ritual that many of us look forward to every year. Although most of the stories in this book and the others in this series, are about bucks with the largest antlers that have been bagged by hunters in Michigan, which helps make them special, they are much more than that.

Some of the stories are about exceptionally old or heavy bucks, too. There's at least one important lesson that can be learned from each story and some of them contain multiple lessons that can be applied to anyone's deer hunting. Some of them are about exceptional luck, as much as anything else. Others are about exceptional skill and still more are about exceptional family hunts. One of the most important points I hope to get across in this book, and that I have strived for in the others, is it is possible for any deer hunter to bag the buck of a lifetime in Michigan without even trying.

It's simply a matter of being in the right place at the right time. Just going deer hunting without any elaborate plans or strategy can be enough to make it happen. That gives each and every hunter who enters our state's deer habitat each and every day of deer season something to look forward to and another reason for being out there.

The best reason to go deer hunting, of course, is simply to spend time in places that whitetails call home. It can be an adventure filled with anticipation, not knowing what you are going to see or experience, but hoping it's interesting, fun and exciting; and it usually is. I enjoy most days of deer hunting, even when I don't see a whitetail, due to the other wildlife I observe and the experience of being in the great outdoors.

The success of someone else on that particular day, whether they are a member of my party or not, is often uplifting and generates optimism for the days that follow. Sharing time afield with those who have similar interests is another great reason to go deer hunting. Great camaraderie can make any deer hunt successful whether or not you bag a deer!

*Aaron Davis with the current state record nontypical bow kill that he got in Hillsdale County on November 14, 2004. The 20-pointer scores 225 7/8.*

# Chapter 1

# *State Record Nontypical Bow Buck*

During the fall of 2004 in Hillsdale County, Aaron Davis of Holland arrowed the highest scoring nontypical on record for the state among bow kills. After being panel measured by Commemorative Bucks of Michigan (CBM), the 20-pointer had an official state record score of 225 7/8, which is four inches more than the green score of 221 7/8 that was arrived at for the rack. Since there are so many measurements on nontypical racks and decisions about which tines are typical versus nontypical can change between green and official scoring, it's not unusual for the final tally to go up.

At least two important judgment calls on the Davis rack played a role in the final scores increasing rather than decreasing. Both brow tines were forked or split, for example. So a determination had to be made about which tines were the brow tines and which were nontypical points arising from them.

The end of the left beam also flared out into three separate projections. Measurers had to determine which was the end of the main beam and whether the others were typical or nontypical points.

Larry Hayes from Hastings was a member of the panel that measured the Davis rack. So were John Knevel from Parma and Duane Temple from Middleton. Both Hayes and Knevel are certified measurers for the Pope and Young Club as well as CBM. Knevel is a

Boone and Crockett scorer, too.

The panel determined that the rack had 11 typical points and nine nontypicals. There were six typical and four nontypical tines on the left antler and five of each on the right side. The longest typical tines were on the left antler; 9 6/8 and 9 3/8 inches in length. The longest nontypical points were on the right antler; 10 5/8 and 9 7/8 inches.

Total length of nontypical points came to 40 inches, which was added to the score. The right beam was 26 inches long and the left was 26 1/8. While the beam tips on most whitetail racks curve inward, the ends of the beams on the Davis Buck flare outward, giving it an impressive inside spread of 25 6/8 inches.

The circumference measurements of the antlers were also impressive. They were all five inches or more. The greatest circumferences of 5 6/8 on the right side and 5 7/8 on the left, were actually between the second and third points.

The rack had a total of seven inches of deductions for differences between the right and left side for typical symmetry. So the gross nontypical score of the antlers was 232 7/8 and the final net score was arrived at by subtracting seven.

Even though the official score of nontypical racks can be higher than the green score, they can also be lower due to shrinkage of antlers, if there's no change in interpretation of typical versus nontypical tines. Davis was concerned about the rack shrinking enough that it might not be a new state record. After all, there was only 2 1/8 inches difference between the green score of his deer and the previous record holder. The previous number one archery nontypical, a 23-pointer scoring 219 6/8, was taken by Bruce Heslet III in Cass County during November of 2000. The story about Heslet's hunt is in Book 4 of this series.

The Davis buck is the first nontypical of Boone and Crockett proportions that qualifies for alltime records listed for Hillsdale County, according to CBM records. Nontypical whitetail antlers have to measure a minimum of 195 to make it into alltime national records maintained by Boone and Crockett, which accepts both gun and bow kills that meet its stringent standards. The highest scoring nontypical on record for the county prior to 2004, according to the

7th edition of "Michigan Big Game Records," is a 16-pointer scoring 191 1/8 that Raymond Fix bagged during the 1995 gun season.

On a statewide basis, the Davis Buck tied for 4th place among all nontypicals taken with gun or bow when this was written in 2009.

Besides the pair of state record bucks (Davis and Bulliner), Hillsdale County gave up another top-ranking whitetail the same year Bulliner got his huge 8-point. On opening day of the 2001 season, Greg McCuiston collected a 15-point typical in the county that currently ranks as the third highest scoring typical in state records with a score of 190 5/8. The McCuiston and Bulliner bucks are the top two typicals for the county. Three more typicals from Hillsdale, all 12-pointers, have measured at least 170, the minimum for entry in alltime B&C records.

The county's reputation for producing big bucks is one reason why Aaron Davis chose to hunt there. He got permission to hunt a large farm about five miles from where Bulliner got his record book buck. The fall of 2004 was his fifth year of hunting the private property and his 13th year of bowhunting.

Davis has been bowhunting since he was 16. His first year of bowhunting for deer was memorable since he got a buck that year on the same weekend as his birthday. His birthday is November 9th.

"My first time in the woods with a bow and arrow, I got a 10-point," Aaron said. "I kinda cursed myself with such quick success. The next couple of years I was deerless. That's when I found out getting a deer with an arrow wasn't as easy as I thought."

The novice bowhunter was sitting on a folding stool at ground level along the edge of an alfalfa field when he got that first buck. He had set up within bow range of a well used trail entering the field. The basket-racked buck came feeding along the edge of the field when Aaron shot it.

Davis arrowed that first buck with the same bow he got the state record with - a Jennings compound with a 70 pound pull. He shoots Game Tracker carbon express arrows out of it, tipped with 100 grain Thunderhead broadheads. The bow is equipped with one sight pin set for 25 yards and Aaron shoots with a Winn Free Flight release.

Besides the 10-point, Davis had taken a button buck and a couple of does with archery equipment prior to the fall of 2004. He said he shot the button buck before he knew how to distinguish young bucks from does. His best gun kill was a decent 7-pointer.

Aaron usually bowhunts with his older brother, Adam, and Adam's friends. He said they may have seen the state record buck prior to 2004 on the farm that they hunt.

"About three years ago (2001), we were tracking a deer my brother shot," Davis said. "It was midday and we were getting ready to head back home, so none of us had our bows with us. Stephen (one of the landowners) was also with us.

"All of a sudden, a big deer appeared in front of us 10 yards away, just looking at us, and no one had a bow. While we stood there staring at this big buck, Stephen muttered something about, 'I can't believe none of you guys has a bow,' trying to be as quiet as possible.

"A year later, I saw what could have easily been the buck I eventually got, running across a field."

Aaron did see the book buck twice during the 2004 season before the day he got it - October 30 and November 6 - each time during the morning. He was hunting a woodlot 30 to 35 acres in size surrounded by large fields planted to corn, soybeans and winter wheat. The interior of the woodlot has cover so thick that he usually hunts the fringes of it.

Davis had a tree stand in the southwest corner of the woodlot, where he's done well in the past. That's where he was posted when he got a glimpse of the trophy buck on October 30 at a distance of 40 yards. Although he saw antlers that morning through an opening in the brush, he didn't get a clear picture of how big they were.

A scouting mission of the northwest corner of the woodlot turned up abundant buck sign, so Aaron was confident the deer was spending a lot of time there and he moved his tree stand to a large oak tree in that vicinity. That's where he was on the morning of November 6 when he got his first good look at the size of the whitetail's antlers, but the buck was still too far for a bow shot.

On the morning of November 14, the day before firearms season, which was a Sunday, Aaron was in the same stand well before daylight.

"I was the only one to make it out that morning because it was 24 degrees," Davis said. "Everyone else stayed in bed. About ten to

8:00, he appeared behind a brushpile where I had seen him before. I could just see his rack moving around. He kept walking away and coming back in. I couldn't figure out what he was doing. Then a doe comes around a corner and I figured out what he was doing.

"He was on her trail. Everywhere she walked, he did. He ended up coming in behind my tree less than 20 yards. I had to turn around in my tree stand. He was quartering away when I shot. He scampered 150 feet and piled up."

About 45 minutes went by from the time Aaron first saw the buck on the morning of November 14 until he released an arrow at it.

"The fact that I had watched him so long, really helped," Davis said. "It helped calm me down. When I took the shot, instinct took over.

"I went to pieces after I made the shot. My legs were shaking and I had to sit down. I was afraid I was going to fall out of the tree stand. I was a nervous wreck.

"After I got the buck, I played a joke on the guys I hunt with," Aaron continued. "I went back to camp and woke everyone up. I told them I shot a nice 6-point. I kept it to myself about the size of the rack until we walked up on it. There was good blood all the way. The guy who saw the buck first accused me of shooting an elk. They had some choice names for me for lying to them. I got the rise out of them I was looking for."

The group who was with Aaron when they found the once-in-a-lifetime buck were his brother, two of Adam's friends and Stephen (one of the land owners). Then the celebration began.

The state record buck is not the only one Davis saw prior to November 14. He saw a 6-point that he passed up. On November 7, he saw a 10 or 12-point that was too far for a good shot. And he almost got a shot at a 10-point on November 12.

"I was almost at full draw on a beautiful, wide 10-point that was coming in on a scent line I left with Tink's 69," Aaron said. "I would have been happy to get that buck. He was one step short of walking into an opening where I had a shot when he noticed a doe in the field and he turned and went to her."

The monster nontypical that Davis did arrow had a dressed weight of 215 pounds. The deer's age has been estimated between 5 1/2 and 7 1/2.

*Dustin Hotchkin with the full mount of his former state record nontypical muzzleloader buck. The Ingham County 17-pointer scores 204 1/8.*

# Chapter 2

# *State Record Nontypical Black Powder Bucks*

Prior to 2004, there was no record of a whitetail with nontypical antlers that would qualify for alltime listing in Boone and Crockett Records (scoring at least 195) having been bagged with a muzzle-loader in Michigan. Then, in 2004, it happened twice.

Dustin Hotchkin from Concord connected on a 17-pointer that grossed 209 5/8 and netted 204 1/8 on Thanksgiving morning, which is during the state's regular gun season. Talk about having something to be thankful for! During the state's 10-day December muzzleloader season, Josh Fritz from Owendale shot a 21-pointer that grossed 204 2/8 and netted 198 4/8.

Either buck would have become the new state record in the nontypical muzzleloader category, but since the Hotchkin buck has the higher scoring antlers, that deer became the state record in that category. Fritz was still happy to be in the number two spot with his deer. During 2007 deer seasons, muzzleloader records changed hands once again. Not only was a nontypical whitetail with antlers scoring more than Hotchkin's bagged with a muzzleloader that year, the bar for typical black powder bucks was also raised. Stories about those deer and how they were taken will most likely be in Book 6 of Great Michigan Deer Tales.

The increasing popularity and dependability of muzzleloaders certainly played a role in the 2004 and 2007 Boone and Crockett double plays in Michigan. During the firearms hunt in the southern third of the state, deer hunters are limited to centerfire shotguns and handguns along with muzzleloaders. The number of hunters who are choosing front loaders over shotguns has been increasing steadily.

The fact that the state has a special black powder deer season, even though it follows the regular gun season and is during December, has also increased the number of hunters afield with muzzleloaders. That season has been in effect since the late 1970s, but participation is still growing.

The bulk of the bucks with the largest antlers are bagged in southern counties each year. Whitetails as young as 3 1/2 are capable of growing world class racks, both typicals and nontypicals. Regardless of the reasons behind it, the taking of a pair of booners with black powder rifles in the same year is worthy of note, especially for the hunters involved. Read on to find out about their hunts.

Dustin was hunting in Ingham County with a .50 caliber Knight Wolverine muzzleloader when he got his state record whitetail on the morning of November 25th. Five inches of fresh snow fell the previous night. Dustin and his younger brother Stetson were excited about the prospects of hunting in fresh snow that day.

Dustin said he never saw the book buck until the day he got it. However, Stetson had seen it four different times. Three of those times were during bow season and a shot was never possible. Stetson saw the buck twice during October and then again on November 11th.

"Each of the times I saw him during bow season, it was always right before dark," Stetson said. "The closest I could get to him was 70 yards."

"The first night Stetson saw the buck he said he saw a 190 class buck," Dustin commented.

When Stetson saw the exceptional whitetail the last time it was on opening day of firearms season at a distance of 150 yards, but he was still unable to get a shot at it.

"When I saw the big buck on November 15th, I had a 6-point and a 4-point right under me," Stetson said. "There were nine does with those bucks. The big buck was at the other end of the woods with eight does. The buck was starting to come down a trail that would have brought him right to me when Dustin came out of the woods to get his knife to gut a doe he shot.

"The deer under me took off and so did the big buck. I climbed down from my tree stand to see if I could get a shot. He made it into a cornfield and we just left him there. We knew of four hunters sitting around the field and we didn't want to push the buck into them."

The state record muzzleloader nontypical came from 300 acres of private property adjoining a large peat bog that the Hotchkins had been managing for six years. Besides the booner that Dustin got, they saw a trio of bucks they figured would score in the 140s and a couple that would score around 125. Other than one day that a friend bowhunted the property, Dustin and Stetson are the only ones who hunt that tract.

On Thanksgiving Day, Dustin said his family had dinner planned for 1:00 p.m., so he decided to hunt until noon. That morning, he climbed into a tree stand on the edge of the woods that was overlooking the intersection of a pair of fields. One of the fields was cut corn and the other was a set aside strip. The stand provided a view of the surrounding woods in addition to the fields.

"I saw him stand up from his bed at 9:00 a.m.," Dustin said. "I thought it was a doe because I couldn't see antlers. They were covered with snow. I watched him for 20 minutes and he just stood there. After about 20 minutes, he shook his head and I decided to turn up the magnification on my scope.

"When I did that, I saw tines on his left side. I thought he was a 10-point I had been seeing. After standing in the one spot for a long time, the buck finally took a couple of steps into an opening. He was angling away at a distance of 120 yards when I took a shot with my .50 caliber Knight rifle. He only went 20 yards and dropped."

Dustin called his brother on a 2-day radio after shooting the buck and they approached the fallen deer together. However, Stetson lagged behind his brother. When Dustin reached the buck and saw it was bigger than he thought, he turned back toward his brother with a surprised look on his face. Stetson knew what that look meant.

"It's that big one, isn't it," Stetson asked.

"Then we hugged and started counting points," Dustin added.

The buck was killed in the same spot where Stetson first saw it during bow season.

"The buck didn't roam very far," Dustin stated. "Each of the spots he was seen in were within 500 yards of where I shot him. When Stetson saw the buck on opening day of gun season, he was the furthest distance from the area where he had been seen the other times."

Dustin said his Knight rifle was loaded with 100 grains of Pyrodex Pellets and a 300 grain Knight red hot bullet. The muzzleloader has a thumb hole stock and was mounted with a 3x-9x Leupold Scope. Hotchkin said percussion caps were the rifle's ignition source when he got it five years earlier, but he eventually modified the gun so 209 shotgun primers could be used to fire it.

"The muzzleloader is all I hunt with in shotgun season anymore," Dustin said. "It's accurate and dependable. I've shot a number of bucks and lots of does with it, but nothing like the one I got during 2004."

Dustin has been deer hunting with a firearm since the legal age of 14 and he was 21 in 2004. He started bowhunting at the age of 15. He got an 11-pointer with bow and arrow during late October of 2004 on a different farm than the one where he shot the state record deer. Hotchkin estimated the antlers on that buck would gross about 110.

Dustin works at Nature's Pride Taxidermy, so he had a full mount done of his record buck. The whitetail was mounted in a bedded position.

### The Fritz Buck

Josh Fritz got his booner on December 17th in Huron County and he didn't have a clue that a buck of those proportions was in the area until the day he got it. He saw the whitetail for the first time the day before he shot it, but even then, he didn't get a true picture of how large its antlers were. Based on the glimpse of the deer he got, he thought the biggest it was was a 10-pointer.

"I never dreamed of ever shooting anything like the one I got up there," Fritz said. "It's pretty incredible for a buck to grow antlers of that size for my area."

The presence of snow and cold weather may have been responsible for Josh being lucky enough to get the buck he did.

"I saw more deer the night I got the big one than I did any other time during the fall," he said. "There were record cold temperatures for our area that day of about 15 degrees and there was three to four inches of snow on the ground."

Josh said 2004 was his 13th year of whitetail hunting. He started bowhunting when he was 12 and began gun hunting two years later. He had taken nine bucks with bow and arrow by the end of 2004 seasons, the biggest of which is a 130-class 10-pointer with an 18-inch spread.

He got that bow buck on October 28, 1998 in the same woods where he got the B&C nontypical.

"That 10-pointer had a big scrape right by my tree stand," Fritz said. "There were 20 buck rubs 50 yards from the tree stand. He came through at 5:00 or 5:15 p.m. He was at the scrape 17 yards away when I shot him. I thought I would never shoot one bigger than that. Guess I was wrong."

The woods where Josh collected both of his best bucks is a 70 acre parcel. He has permission to hunt 25 acres of it. He was hunting from an enclosed ground blind when he got the booner. The blind was a lot more comfortable in the cold weather than a tree stand would have been.

A pair of well used runways are within view of the blind. A couple of nearby oak trees produce acorns that attract hungry whitetails. Josh also puts some corn out as incentive for deer to feed in the area.

If Fritz had gotten in his blind earlier on December 16th, he may have put his tag on the buck that day instead of the 17th. It was 4:00 p.m. that day by the time he got close to his blind.

"I got out kinda late after work on Thursday, December 16th," Josh said. "As I was walking about 50 yards from the blind I saw two deer get up. One of them was a buck. He got up with a doe and ran away.

"I knew it was at least an 8 or 10-point. I didn't see all of the smaller points on the rack. I thought my chances of seeing him again were pretty well shot after spooking him like that."

Fortunately, he was wrong about that. Even though Josh thought the odds of seeing the buck again were against him, he wasn't willing to quit hunting. He figured there were other bucks in the area. To decrease the chances of spooking deer on the way to his blind the following day, he decided to get in position earlier.

Fritz was hunting with a .50 caliber CVA Apollo muzzleloader that was loaded with 90 grains of Pyrodex Powder and a saboted 285 grain bullet. The rifle was fitted with a Bushnell 3x-9x scope that was sighted in for 100 yards. Based on practice with the rifle and load, Josh knew his bullets dropped three inches at 130 yards.

He said he had taken a couple of does with the front loader. He also shot a 6-pointer during the regular gun season with it on November 22nd. He had both the muzzleloader and a shotgun with him that day. He took a 140 yard shot at the 6-pointer, hitting it low.

When the buck took off after the shot, Josh grabbed his shotgun to followup on the deer with rather than reloading the black powder rifle. When he caught up to the whitetail, he finished it with the shotgun.

*Photo courtesy Josh Fritz*

*Josh Fritz with his Huron County nontypical muzzleloader kill.*
*The B&C 21-pointer nets 198 4/8.*

"I saw a total of 13 does and fawns on the 17th," Fritz said. "The deer were really moving. All of the deer activity helped the time go by. There were three does in front of me when it was getting close to 4:30 p.m. They took off and the buck came out five minutes later.

"I only watched him for about two minutes before shooting. He was 40 yards away facing me. I would have preferred a broadside shot, but I was afraid he was going to take off, so I took the shot I had. My scope was set on 9 power, so I aimed carefully.

"He ran about 50 yards and dropped. He went over a ridge, so he was out of my sight, but I did hear crashing in the brush, so I thought he had gone down. I started reloading the rifle and I had a hard time of it. I kept dropping things."

Both the cold and excitement about having shot a good buck contributed to the difficulty in reloading the muzzleloader. After the rifle was finally reloaded, Josh walked up on the ridge that the buck had gone over after being hit. From that vantage point, he could see the whitetail where it had fallen.

"I thought it was just maybe a nice 8-point or 10-point," Josh commented. "I didn't know it was a 21-pointer. When I got to the deer I couldn't believe how many points there were. It was unbelievable!

"I counted the points and I got it right. I called it a 21-pointer. I wasn't sure what qualified as a point, but I still came up with the right number.

"After I got the deer, I talked to a guy who thinks he shot at the same buck on the 15th," Fritz continued. "He was only hunting about 200 yards from where I shot the whitetail, so it easily could have been. He was pretty excited."

Fortunately for Josh, the other hunter's shot missed. Fritz said there were no other fresh wounds on the buck. However, the deer had been hit by a load of buckshot, perhaps the year before.

One of the buckshot pellets had broken the buck's right jaw, but that break had fully healed. Another pellet was found behind the right shoulder, but that pellet was just under the skin, so it hadn't done any damage. The buck was apparently too far from the shooter to do serious damage.

The booner was aged at 4 1/2 or 5 1/2 years old and had a dressed weight of 170 pounds. The rack has a typical 11-point frame. There are 10 tines on the right side, four of which are nontypicals and 11 on the left, six of which are nontypicals. Total length of nontypical points is 34 7/8 inches.

*Jeanetta Flanery with her state record nontypical bow kill among women. The Livingston County 16-pointer measures 185 5/8.*

# Chapter 3

# Milestones For Women

New high marks for whitetail antlers among women in the world of Michigan deer hunting were set during 2003 and 2006. In 2003, Barb Loy from Schoolcraft bagged a Kalamazoo County 13-pointer during the December muzzleloader season that is a state record in the typical muzzleloader category among women. During October of 2006, Jeanetta Flanery from Fenton arrowed a Livingston County 16-pointer that is a state record in the nontypical archery listings for women.

Like many dedicated bow deer hunters, Flanery was trying to squeeze in some hunting time on the morning of October 7, 2006 before going to work. At the time, she was hoping to see some deer and possibly get a shot at a buck from her tree stand. The thoughts of arrowing a state record whitetail never crossed her mind, but that's what she did that morning and she accomplished the feat before even reaching her stand.

The large, beautiful rack from the 16-pointer she got that day has a gross score of 188 3/8 and nets 185 5/8, which is high enough to qualify for national records maintained by the Pope and Young and Boone and Crockett Clubs besides a top spot in state records. Nontypical bow kills only have to score 125 to make it into state records compiled by Commemorative Bucks of Michigan (CBM). The minimum entry scores for Pope and Young and Boone and Crockett are 150 and 185 respectively.

The previous state record nontypical among female archers was a 17-pointer scoring 173 1/8 that Linda Luna collected in Genesee County during 1993. The story behind Linda's buck can be found in Book 2 of Great Michigan Deer Tales. In an amazing coincidence, another woman arrowed a trophy nontypical that was similar in size to the Luna Buck on the same day that Jeanetta got her state record deer. Kelly Hatch was hunting in Washtenaw County on the evening of October 7th when she connected on a whopper 16-pointer. Her deer netted 164 1/8 and had a gross score of 172.

Hatch was hunting from a tree stand when the buck came along. She started counting points and when she got up to five and realized there were still more, she decided she had better shoot the deer and finish counting later. That's what she did. A second buck with a rack similar in size to the one she got was with it.

The Flanery Buck will rank fifth among nontypicals on record for Livingston County, according to the 7th edition of Michigan Big Game Records published by CBM. The county's top two nontypicals were taken by male bowhunters. Michel (Mick) LaFountain arrowed a 20-pointer netting 209 5/8 in 2000 and Patrick Harris tagged a 23-pointer netting 195 5/8 in 1995. The story behind LaFountain's buck can be found elsewhere in this book. The Harris Buck is covered in Book 2 of this series.

The fall of 2006 was Flanery's seventh year of bowhunting for whitetails. She had taken two other bucks with archery equipment prior to that fall. Her first buck, an 8-pointer she thinks was a yearling, was taken during her first year of bowhunting in 2000.

After listening to her husband, brothers and father-in-law talk about their bowhunting experiences, Jeanetta's husband talked her into trying it one day during the summer of 2000 when they were in a sporting goods store. They bought all of the equipment she needed that day. She got her first buck ever that fall as a first time bowhunter.

She nailed her second buck, a 7-pointer, in 2002. That one would have also been an 8-point if it weren't for a broken tine on the left side.

Jeanetta said she could have shot smaller bucks, but her family has a rule about passing up young bucks. If they want meat, they shoot a doe instead of a spike, forkhorn or small 6-point. They pass on young bucks with small antlers.

Flanery started deer hunting with a rifle when she was 16, so she had hunted whitetails with firearms for 30 years by 2006, but she had not yet shot a buck with a rifle. She had taken three does during gun season, however. Her first deer ever was a doe that she dropped at a distance of more than 100 yards with an iron sighted .30-30.

The morning of October 7, 2006 was not the first time Jeanetta saw the buck she put her tag on. The deer was feeding on apples from trees in her yard when its antlers were still in velvet. They obtained a trail camera photo of him in August. Based on examination of that photograph, she thought the whitetail had 12 points.

After the photo was taken in August, Flanery said she saw the buck on two other occasions before hunting season opened. She spends a lot of time monitoring deer activity on the property she and her husband own, so she's familiar with their movement patterns. That knowledge came in handy on the morning of October 7th as she headed for her tree stand.

Jeanetta's hike toward her stand was interrupted by the sound of antlers. Two sets of antlers from bucks that were sparring.

"I slowly and cautiously worked my way toward the sound to try to get a glimpse of the bucks," Flanery said. "I snuck over to some pines that would provide some cover. After looking around I finally spotted two deer and one was a big buck.

"I maneuvered for a better look, doing my best not to spook them. I watched them stand there out of bow range at a distance of 250 feet. I was excited about the possibility of getting a shot at one of the bucks, if they would only come my way.

"My excitement turned to disappointment," Jeanetta continued, "when I saw them turn and start to walk away from me instead of toward me. But I wasn't disappointed for long. Somebody started a vehicle in the direction the bucks were going, which suddenly spooked them back my way.

"I prepared myself for a possible shot and waited for them to appear, and then waited some more. It seemed like it was taking them longer than expected to reappear. I hoped they didn't change directions again.

"Finally, one of the bucks suddenly appeared and walked around the end of a fence 50 feet away. What an adrenaline rush! All I could hear was my heart pounding. I began shaking and couldn't breathe.

"Fortunately, drawing my bow had a calming effect. It forced me to focus on the familiar routine of aiming to make an accurate shot. I aimed for the heart and released. My arrow hit a little high, but I knew I still made a good shot."

The fact that the buck was down within 80 feet confirmed the arrow was well placed. The distance the arrowed whitetail traveled after the hit was reduced, no doubt, because it slammed into the fence it walked around moments earlier. The force of the whitetail hitting the fence broke four posts off at ground level.

Jeanetta said she had feelings of shock and disbelief about what happened after it was over. She shot the buck with a 45 pound pull Hoyt Sport Rebel XT bow that has a 65 percent letoff at full draw. She was shooting aluminum arrows tipped with 4-blade, 90 grain Wasp broadheads. Her bow is fitted with one sight pin set for 35 yards. She shoots her bow with bare fingers, not using a glove or tab.

The buck was 4 1/2 or 5 1/2 years old. After shooting the deer, Flanery talked to someone who has trail camera photos of the buck over a three year period; 2004 through 2006. But what many people don't realize, is the buck that Jeanetta shot was the smaller of the two that she heard sparring.

The one she didn't get is the one she thought was a big buck, although the one she ended up shooting proved to be bigger than she thought it was. The Flanery Buck is a main frame 10-point, with three sticker points more than an inch long on the bases of the antlers.

"The main frame on the buck my deer was sparring with was at least a 10 like the one I got," Jeanetta wrote, "but it was much bigger, wider and taller. It was definitely bigger."

It's clear from Flanery's description that the second buck most likely had antlers large enough to qualify for alltime listing in Boone and Crockett Records. Since her whitetail scored in the 180s, it's safe to conclude the other deer would have measured at least in the 190s.

Jeanetta said the feeling of taking a buck of the caliber she did is like winning the lottery. She also had a hard time believing the antlers were of state record proportions when CBM's Lonnie Buck measured them.

"A lot of people hunt all their lives and may never get the opportunity I got that morning," Flanery wrote, "but it just goes to show you that you never know when a chance and luck may happen. Hunting is relaxing as well as exciting and a great gift. Just seeing the woods come to life in the morning and anticipating what could come by you are a couple of the reasons I hunt."

She hopes her story motivates other women to try deer hunting.

### Black Powder Buck

Barb Loy from Schoolcraft has been deer hunting since she was 14 years old. Over the 21 years she hunted whitetails through 2003, she had bagged eight bucks, two of which were tagged during 2003 seasons. Both of the antlered whitetails she shot in 2003 were her biggest ever.

The larger of the two was not only her best buck, its antlers are large enough to be a new state record in the typical muzzleloader category among women. The 13-pointer she got in Kalamazoo County on December 18th has a gross score of 171 1/8 and nets 164 6/8.

The previous state record typical black powder buck among women was taken by Esther Frantom in Branch County on November 17, 1998. The 10-pointer that she got on the third day of the regular firearms season that year netted 163. The story about Frantom's buck is in Book 3 of Great Michigan Deer Tales.

Both of the bucks Barb got during 2003 were taken while posted along the edge of a bean field that attracts numerous whitetails. She scored on her first one during the regular firearms season. It was the evening of November 21 when she was occupying a tree stand at the end of the field with her Remington 870 12 gauge shotgun loaded with 000 buckshot.

The 9-pointer was on the edge of a nearby swamp at a distance of 25 yards when Barb dropped him. That 2 1/2-year-old whitetail weighed 166 pounds and was her best buck up to that point.

That all changed on the evening of December 18. Late that afternoon, she and her 11-year-old son James went to her father's ground blind on the edge of the bean field. It's a Shadow Hunter Blind manufactured in Marcellus.

A pair of rack bucks had already been taken from that blind

during gun season. Barb's mother, Marylou Sagers, shot a 9-pointer from the blind on the morning of November 15. Barb's father, Ron, connected on a 10-pointer later on during the season.

Besides borrowing her father's blind, Barb also used his .50 caliber Knight Muzzleloader to hunt with. The rifle was mounted with a 3X-9X Burris Scope, was loaded and ready to go. The load consisted of 100 grains of powder and a Power Belt bullet.

As the sun dropped toward the horizon, plenty of whitetails started appearing in the bean field to feed. Most of them were does and fawns, but there were a pair of small bucks with spike antlers. A third buck had forked antlers.

"Around 5:00 p.m., three huge bucks came out of the swamp to eat in the bean field," Barb said. "I could not believe how big all three were. When I pulled up the gun and scope, I picked the middle one to shoot. He had a nice big rack."

The bucks were about 75 yards away when Barb shot. All three of the deer ran down the field toward where Loy's husband was posted in another blind, but only two of them made it. It would have been fitting if John Loy could have collected one of the other bucks since it was his birthday, but, unfortunately, he was not able to get a good shot at the running whitetails.

"I knew my buck was big," Barb commented, "but I didn't realize just how exceptional he was until my dad and brother made a big deal about his rack. I was just glad to have gotten him. Then I had a lot of fun having the antlers measured and attending a number of shows. I even got invited to Big Buck Night at Outdoorama in Novi and was interviewed on stage by Bob Garner for the Michigan Out-of-Doors TV Show."

No one had seen this buck previously, so it may have just moved into the area or it had been primarily nocturnal until then. The buck was 3 1/2 years old and had a dressed weight of 155 pounds. The buck was lighter than the younger 9-point she got in November because the 13-pointer was an active participant in the rut and he had another month to lose weight from chasing does.

The antlers from Barb's buck had exceptional brow tines. In fact, they were the longest tines on the rack, which is unusual. The right brow tine was 10 6/8 inches long and the left one was 9 7/8 inches in length. The second tine on the right side was 9 3/8 inches long and the third one measured 9 inches. The G2 and 3 tines on the left antler were 8 3/8 and 8 inches long. The rack has a typical 12-point frame, with a short nontypical point measuring 1 1/8 inches off the left brow tine.

The right beam measured 21 6/8 inches and the left was 23 2/8. Inside spread of the antlers was 17 5/8 inches. Circumferences of the base of each antler was the same at 4 6/8 inches.

*Photo courtesy Barb Loy*

*Barb Loy with her state record muzzleloader buck among women. The Kalamazoo County 13-point taped 164 6/8.*

*John Benedict with the 17-point nontypical scoring 192 7/8 that
he successfully bagged with bow and arrow during 2005
after missing it the year before.*

## Chapter 4

# More Book Bucks For Benedict

The last chapter in Book 4 of Great Michigan Deer Tales was about the exceptional ground based bowhunting success for book bucks by John Benedict from Auburn Hills. That chapter covered his success on whitetails in Michigan through the fall of 2004. This chapter takes up where the one in Book 4 left off.

Benedict continues his impressive string of bagging record book bucks with bow and arrow from the ground. Through 2008 seasons, he had entered 40 whitetails in state records maintained by Commemorative Bucks of Michigan (CBM) from a total of 27 different counties and 17 of those deer also qualify for entry in national archery records kept by the Pope and Young Club. The rest of the story is especially appropriate since there's an important connection between the biggest buck John arrowed in 2004 and his best bow kill in 2005.

That year (2005) was the fourth year in a row that Benedict bagged one of the highest scoring bow kills measured by CBM from each of those years. On the evening of October 30, 2005, Benedict arrowed a 17-point nontypical in Eaton County that has a gross score of 198 5/8 and nets 192 7/8, making it the second highest scoring nontypical bow kill known taken in Michigan during 2005.

During the fall of 2004, John got a bow shot at a big nontypical in Eaton County from which he had found the previous year's shed antlers. John's arrow hit a sapling instead of its intended target. Since the errant arrow didn't appear to spook the rutting whitetail,

Benedict continued hunting the area, hoping for another chance at it.

He didn't get the nontypical he missed. Instead, he arrowed a Boone and Crockett qualifying typical 10-point on which the antlers grossed 175 4/8 and netted 171. In 2005, John resumed his hunt for the nontypical that escaped him the year before on the same farm and was successful.

The antlers from Benedict's 2005 nontypical buck easily qualified for a place in national archery records maintained by the Pope and Young Club as well as the honorable mention category in Boone and Crockett Records. The fall of 2005 marked the seventh year in a row that John collected at least one bow buck from Michigan that exceeds Pope and Young minimums. Antlers from bucks he's arrowed exceeded Boone and Crockett minimums over the course of four years.

When this was written in 2009, Benedict's nontypical bow kill from 2005 was the highest scoring nontypical taken with archery equipment on record for Eaton County, according to CBM. It was the number two nontypical taken with any weapon for the county. The county's number one nontypical is a 25-pointer netting 203 7/8 that Mark Janousek dropped with a handgun during the 1991 gun season. The story behind Mark's B&C handgun kill can be found in Book 1 of Great Michigan Deer Tales.

The 17-pointer wasn't the only book buck John got with bow and arrow in 2005. During late December, he arrowed a second Pope and Young buck in Lapeer County on property leased by the American Sportsmen's Club. The Lapeer County whitetail had an 8-point rack that grossed 148 5/8 and netted 145 1/8.

The private property in Eaton County where John got top end bucks two years in a row consists of 40 acres with a 25-acre woodlot. When John scouted the woodlot during the spring of 2004, he salvaged the largest set of shed antlers he had ever found in the state, up to that time. Those sheds prompted him to plan on hunting the property during the fall of 2004. He returned to the spot during early summer to prepare a pair of ground blinds.

Benedict prefers to hunt from the ground with bow and arrow as a result of a fall he suffered from a tree stand a number of years ago. He normally uses natural material to construct blinds and he's done

**34**

extremely well from ground-based positions. He has a knack for that type of hunting.

"I picked out one spot in the northeast corner of the woods that overlooked a cornfield," John wrote, "and another location deeper in the woods along a main trail from the corn to the bedding area. The first spot was at the intersection of a ridge that ran through the field and the woodline. I constructed a couple of rudimentary ground blinds using branches and debris from recent windstorms and cut a few shooting lanes.

"The area where the ridge intersected the woods seemed to be the most likely point for a buck to enter the field. A few steps into the field would put him in the only spot that gave an unobstructed view of the entire field. So my plan was to use this blind."

Benedict was in that blind on Halloween evening during 2004 and it worked as well as he hoped it would in terms of putting him in position for a shot at the buck that had lost the antlers he found. Unfortunately, as mentioned earlier, an unseen sapling intercepted John's arrow before it connected with the whitetail in the fading light. John returned to the same blind on November 1st and that's when he got the 10-pointer.

Those same two blinds were ready for use during the 2005 bow season. John simply retrimmed shooting lanes and the path to the blinds. Some large antler rubs in the vicinity confirmed a mature buck was still in the area and John suspected it was the one he had missed the year before.

On the Monday after opening day of bow season, John hunted the parcel with the exceptional antler rubs.

"By nightfall, I had seen three young bucks and at least 20 does and fawns," Benedict wrote in an email. "The biggest buck was a beautiful eight or nine point. You could tell by his body size and shape that he was an 18-month old deer. His rack didn't have much mass, but the spread was a good 15 inches.

"I didn't see the deer I was after, but there was plenty of evidence that he was still around. The trees he chose to rub were all in the 7 to 8-inch diameter variety, and he left a distinctive path of destruction. His rubs were so impressive that I made one more visit to hunt on the second weekend of the season.

"Again, I passed on a buck that was in the 110-inch range. This one was a young 8-pointer traveling the main ridge trail that bisected the cornfield. I decided to leave this property alone until I was sure the rut was underway. Some of the new rubs I saw that day were clearly from a large aggressive buck, and one was 10 yards from my best blind."

John didn't hunt that property again until October 29th. He planned on hunting as hard as possible for three days. He expected to see bucks chasing does all day and he did.

"The problem was that the bucks I saw were all young or had broken antlers," Benedict wrote. "One guy had a main beam broken off just above the brow tine. That break took serious effort to accomplish, which was more evidence that a big, aggressive buck was in the area.

"I saw five bucks and a minimum of 30 doe. I'm sure I passed up 'chip shots' at two bucks and at least five doe. I had four scent canisters surrounding my blind at a distance of 20 yards and all but one got knocked over by doe sniffing them."

John returned to the same blind on the morning of the 30th, which was a Sunday. He had seen 16 deer by 9:00 a.m., when he took a break to go to church, but none of them had antlers. During the afternoon, he saw a young buck chasing a doe and the buck with the broken antler eating acorns.

"As light started to fade for the day, I was contemplating the best course of action for the morning," John recalled, "when the noise of running deer caught my attention. Seconds later, a big doe trotted into view on the trail. She stopped 20 yards out and turned to look back. I readied my bow for the draw in case a buck was on her heels. Sure enough, he was only a few seconds behind her. She let him get within sniffing distance before she took off again.

"I could have reached out and touched her as she passed, but my eyes were 100 percent on the bruiser buck that came to a standstill 10 yards from the blind. His rack was dark and massive enough to signal 'shooter' without having to count points. He broke off his pursuit long enough to check out the field from his ridge top vantage point.

"When he turned away, I drew, and when he came back to a

quartering away angle, I released. The arrow entered behind the ribs and angled toward the far shoulder. He bucked, did a 180 degree turn and headed back into the bedding thicket. I heard him for a while before things got quiet, except for the doe snorting at me from downwind and the pack of coyotes yipping up a storm over by the river bottom."

John decided to eat dinner before taking up the deer's trail. Unraveling the blood trail in the dark proved more time consuming than expected due to fallen leaves with natural red splotches on them and the blood sign was sparse. He finally found the buck at 10:30 p.m. The fact that his broadhead had lodged in the buck's right shoulder instead of exiting, contributed to the poor blood trail.

## 2006-2008

The two bucks Benedict bagged with bow and arrow in Michigan during 2006 scored 108 6/8 and 140 4/8. The bigger of the two had 12 points. Due to hunts in another state, Benedict only arrowed one book buck in Michigan during 2007. Its antlers netted 141 2/8.

In 2008, John had another banner year. He bow bagged a pair of bucks, one with nontypical antlers and the other with typical antlers, that are among the highest scoring in each category for the year.

The nontypical is an 18-pointer that was arrowed in Hillsdale County on November 12, 2008 that scores 170 6/8. The typical is a 11-pointer from Shiawassee County that was bagged on October 27, 2008 and nets 164 3/8. Both bucks also qualify for national archery records maintained by the Pope and Young Club and the typical is big enough to make it into national records maintained by the Boone and Crockett Club, too.

In most cases, the experienced bowhunter sees a buck he's interested in trying for and then does his best to get permission to hunt the property where the deer lives. Then he patterns the whitetail as best as he can before hunting that specific animal.

The 18-point nontypical Benedict collected in 2008, however, was an exception. He didn't expect to shoot any deer the day he got that one because he was trying to help a prospective member of the American Sportsmen's Club score on a property leased by the club in Hillsdale County. The property only has an 18 acre woodlot, according to John, with a bean field to the north, stubble field to the west, residence on the south and highway along the eastern border.

Before daylight on the 12th of November, Benedict led the bow-hunter to a ladder stand in the center of the woodlot and then selected a spot in the northwest corner of the woods to stand on the ground where he knew his presence would not interfere with his guest's hunt. John was a few yards inside the edge of the woods where he had some cover. He had his bow and arrows with him, just in case, and it's a good thing he did.

Although John had not seen the big buck that frequented this property, other club members had, so he knew about its presence. He had seen a large antler rub that was most likely made by the buck.

"About two hours into the morning, it started to rain and things started to happen," John wrote. "A doe and fawn came down the west border of the property and wandered into the woods directly toward the stand in the center. Then I heard a truck hit the brakes on the road that borders the property, and saw movement in the beans by the road. A large buck was at a full run headed into the northeast corner of the woods.

"I could visualize that buck running into the heart of the woods and giving my guest an exciting morning, but the deer had a different route in mind. He must have taken a hard left as soon as he hit the woods and gotten onto the trail that paralleled the edge of the woods. This trail came within 10 yards of my impromptu ground blind.

"I heard the buck break a stick as he worked his way toward me," John continued, "but the brush hid him until he got within 40 yards. It seemed to take forever for him to move the next few yards, but he finally came into view. He had triple brow tines on each side, mass, and more than enough tine length to make him a 'shooter' in anyone's book. He also had a gray muzzle, big body, and a belly that made him look pregnant.

"This all registered in a couple of nanoseconds, and the next minute or two sped by like a galloping glacier. He stopped, raised his tail to half mast, stuck his nose into the air as far up as he could reach, and then turned directly away from me. I was afraid my scent had swirled around to him, but he made a full circle back to the trail and continued in my direction.

"When he was about fifteen yards out, I got the opportunity

to draw. My bow scraped a branch as I drew and he immediately jumped off the trail a couple of bounds. He was now quartering away, headed back the way he had come. He stopped at about 20 yards and I figured it was now or never, and released the arrow.

"I aimed low because the buck was very alert, and as he crouched for his get away bound, the arrow caught him just behind the rib cage and angled into his left shoulder on the far side. I must have hit bone because the buck ran off with the fletching still protruding from his right side."

As it turned out, the buck dropped within view of the hunter in the ladder stand, who had seen four does and a 6-point before the buck John arrowed. Needless to say, John's guest had an exciting morning.

The hunt for the Shiawassee County typical that John nailed on October 27th is more "typical" of how Benedict connects on book bucks. He spotted the trophy whitetail from his vehicle while driving toward home on a highway after visiting relatives. He then secured permission to hunt the farm where he had seen the buck and did some long distance scouting with a spotting scope on the second week of September.

Five bucks stepped into a field he was watching just before dark. The largest of them had a main frame 10-point rack with some stickers. That was the one he had seen earlier and the one he wanted to collect with an arrow.

The first time John hunted the farm on October 14 he posted in a ground blind he fashioned from a blowdown, but the disturbance from preparing the spot to hunt must have alerted the local deer because he didn't see any whitetails within bow range. When he returned a week later, he found out the buck he was after was the only one not using the trail his blind overlooked. The trophy whitetail came in on a trail behind his blind and winded him, blowing loudly when the deer detected danger.

Fortunately, the buck as well as nearby antlerless deer, were not too badly spooked. The buck "stopped and began feeding as though nothing happened after getting 50 yards into the field," John reported. He added that, "Eight doe had also moved into the field, and were beginning to calm down."

When Benedict returned to the farm on the 27th, he spent the morning in the blowdown blind, witnessing a sparring match between a 6-point and 8-point with a broken brow tine. Around noon, he checked out the area where the big buck busted him on the previous hunt, finding a trail with big tracks on it. He decided to move to a spot overlooking that trail.

"The only cover was large tree trunks," he wrote, "so there would not be a blind of any sort, just a stand in a strategic spot. I found a good spot, but it was covered-up with sticks and leaves and rose stickers. I had trimmers in my fanny pack, so was able to quietly cut back the whips of rose and small branches, but needed to clear a quiet place to stand.

"My approach to this task is to stage a buck fight with the rattle bag and grunt call while scraping away the leaves and small sticks from the area near the tree I have picked for cover. It works well and makes for a realistic sounding scuffle. As with most hunting situations, the idea is not to have total silence, but to have whatever noise is made be natural and unthreatening."

Just before 2:00 p.m., John was ready for action in the new spot. He thought about retrieving the stool he had been sitting on from the blowdown ground blind, but decided against it because the rut was in progress and he knew bucks could be on the prowl at any time. And the buck fight he had staged while preparing the new spot might have also caught the attention of a nearby buck. It's a good thing he remained where he was because a half hour later he detected the presence of a deer in a nearby thicket and a couple of soft grunts got the desired results.

"When he cleared the thick stuff, and got onto the trail, I centered him on the far side of the tree, drew my bow, and eased around to where I could see his progress," John wrote. "He stopped at 35 yards, which is a long shot for me, so I waited (in a steady rain). Luckily, he started moving again and closed to about twenty yards.

"I made a soft bleat to stop him, and touched off the release. It was a broadside, double lung shot, with the arrow passing through and sticking into a tree 10 yards on the other side of the deer. The buck spun around and crashed back into the thicket, and I heard him go down within seconds."

Steady rain quickly turned into a downpour, so John didn't wait before following up on the buck. A continuous blood trail that was still intact made it easy to locate the whitetail, but it took him two hours to drag and field dress the carcass. It was raining hard the entire time, so John was soaking wet by the time he secured the deer.

Although the rack has several stickers, only one nontypical point is long enough to be considered an official point. Both of Benedict's book bucks from 2008 had dressed weights close to 190 pounds. The 11-pointer was a few pounds heavier. The whitetails were at least 3 1/2 years old.

*Photo courtesy John Benedict*

*John got this 11-pointer in Shiawassee County on October 27, 2008. The antlers net 164 3/8.*

*Richard and Paul Barton with the trophy nontypical they both shot with bow and arrow in Genesee County.*

## Chapter 5

# *The Barton Buck*

A huge 19-point nontypical from Genesee County that was taken with bow and arrow during the fall of 2003 was destined to be listed in the record books under the name Barton. On the morning of October 26, brothers Richard and Paul Barton were occupying commercial pop-up ground blinds about 70 yards apart and the exceptional whitetail ended up in front of both of them. Each of the archers put an arrow into the deer, unaware that the other had also scored a hit on the buck.

Both hits were fatal. However, if either arrow had missed, the buck still would have belonged to a Barton. The huge rack grossed 194 5/8 and nets 191 1/8 as a nontypical. If scored as a typical, the antlers would have only netted 165.

The buck is the highest scoring nontypical taken with bow and arrow from Genesee County, according to CBM records in 2009 and ranked second overall among nontypicals from the county. Another 19-pointer collected in the county with a shotgun during 2000 by Matthew Caudill is the number one nontypical for the county. Those antlers measured 200 1/8.

Even though both brothers made killing shots on the buck, there was no controversy about who should tag the deer. Richard arrowed the whitetail first, so he is listed as the successful hunter in state records.

"Paul said I deserved to tag the deer," Richard commented. "I was working out of state for the previous four years and didn't get to hunt that much. Besides, I'm older than he is," he added with a chuckle.

The monster buck is the second antlered whitetail to Richard's credit during 25 years of deer hunting. His first buck was taken 25 years earlier on opening day of firearms season. He was hunting with a 16 gauge shotgun loaded with 00 buckshot.

"I didn't expect to even see anything the day I got my first buck," Richard said. "It came up behind me in a cornfield. I could hear it coming. I shot him when he was 40 feet away."

The buck was an 8-pointer that weighed about 150 pounds.

The Barton brothers started bowhunting for deer at least nine years before getting the book buck. Over that time, they had each taken does with bow and arrow. They hunt on 30 acres of land with two other people.

The Bartons started seeing a big buck feeding in a nearby bean-field during the summer and Richard spent a lot of time watching it.

"I couldn't really tell how many points he had or the exact dimensions of the rack," Barton said. "The beans grew pretty tall and I could only see the top of his antlers most of the time. I was a long distance away, too. I watched him from more than 300 yards away. The binoculars I looked at him with weren't the best either."

Of course, Richard didn't need to know exactly how big the rack was for him to know he would like to get the deer during bow season. He knew the antlers were bigger than anything else he had ever seen and that was good enough for him. Presence of the trophy whitetail served as incentive for him to do a lot of practicing with his 70 pound pull Darton bow. He also had a new string put on his bow to prepare for the upcoming season.

Due to the fact 2003 was the first year Richard was back home in Michigan after living out of state, was another reason he looked forward to bow season. He planned on doing more hunting than he had been able to during the previous four years. He came home to hunt each of those four years, but his hunting time was limited due to the travel involved and his work schedule.

The Bartons have a pair of white shacks on stilts on their hunting land, according to Paul. He said one is elevated 10 feet and the other is 14 feet above the ground. They also use a pair of portable, pop-up commercial blinds that allow them the flexibility to move around quickly and easily to different parts of the property.

"We use the portable ground blinds to go where we see scrapes and things like that," Paul said. "When it's raining is primarily when we go in the elevated shacks."

On opening day of the 2003 bow season, Paul saw a big buck while hunting from one of the shacks.

"Right at daybreak, I saw a big buck sparring with a 4-point," Paul said. "They were 50 yards away. I think it was pop and his son. The bigger buck was teaching the youngster how to fight. I had six does underneath me at the time.

"It was fun to watch the bucks, but they were too far for a shot. They never came any closer."

Paul was pretty sure the buck he saw on the morning of October 1 was the same one they had seen during the summer in the beanfield.

The brothers were in their portable ground blinds at first light on October 26. Richard's blind was in a swale. He had just finished eating a snack size Snickers candy bar and was putting the wrapper in his pocket when a big whitetail suddenly appeared. The time was 7:10 a.m. The deer hadn't made a sound to alert the bowhunter of its presence.

"The buck came walking by me and stopped at 30 yards," Barton said. "He looked back to the right when he stopped. I could see the deer had antlers right away. I didn't bother to try to count points or anything. I just decided to shoot it and I did."

Richard's 70 pound pull bow only has one sight pin set for 40 yards. Since the arrows he shoots out of the bow have a flat trajectory, the sight is on at any distance out to 40 yards. He also uses a peep sight and a release.

His arrow was tipped with an expandable Spitfire broadhead. Richard saw the arrow connect and he felt good about the shot. Seconds later, the same buck stopped in front of brother Paul's blind, also at a distance of 30 yards.

"I couldn't tell that my brother had already shot the deer," Paul said. "The deer was standing in high weeds, so I couldn't see an arrow or any blood. The only thing on my mind when I saw the buck was to shoot it and I did."

Paul was hunting with a 60 pound pull Oneida bow. His arrow was tipped with a 125 grain Thunderhead.

"I was excited about having shot a big buck and pretty soon Richard came along and asked, 'Where did my buck go?' I then said, You're buck?, totally surprised about what he said. It took us a while to realize we both shot the same buck.

"We waited a half hour to 45 minutes before looking for the deer. It went another 60 yards after I shot it. We were both in awe about how big the antlers were. We were grateful to finally get him in our possession."

Richard said it's tough to put into words how he felt when they walked up to the fallen buck. He described it as an "awesome" moment. They counted the points on the deer's antlers and came up with 20. One of the tines ended up being less than an inch in length, eliminating it from consideration when the rack was officially measured by CBM scorer Tom O'Brien.

The antlers had a green net score of 195 4/8, so the antlers shrunk approximately 4 3/8 inches during the drying period. The buck had a dressed weight between 200 and 220 pounds. The scale they weighed him on had 20-pound increments. The deer was aged at 5 1/2.

The brothers eventually decided that the buck they both shot on October 26 was bigger than the one they had been watching during the summer. One of the features that helped them make that decision are the brow tines. Both brow tines are split on the deer they got, but not the one they were watching during the summer.

The buck that Paul saw on October 1 is the one they had been seeing in the beanfield. After becoming familiar with how much the antlers scored on the buck they got, Paul guessed the smaller antlers would score in the 160s as a nontypical. The brothers were more than happy to settle for a whitetail with about 30 inches more antler than the buck they had been after. Who wouldn't be?

*Photo courtesy Richard Barton*

*Richard Barton with the buck he arrowed before it went by his brother. Since he drew first blood, he tagged the deer.*

*Tim Sauter (right) and Todd Perin with the trophy buck they
both shot in Lenawee County.*

## Chapter 6

# Michigan's Most
# Massive Antlers

A huge 12-point typical whitetail that Mitch Rompola of Traverse City got with bow and arrow on November 11, 1998, grabbed many of the deer hunting headlines during the months that followed (refer to Books 3 and 4 of Great Michigan Deer Tales for detailed coverage about the Rompola Buck). There was another trophy buck bagged in the state days later that also proved to be controversial, but for a different reason. That deer was taken in Lenawee County on November 16 and its antlers have more mass than any other whitetail listed in state records, according to former Commemorative Bucks of Michigan (CBM) spokesperson Tira O' Brien.

She said the 17-point nontypical rack has a gross score of 197 5/8 and netted 180 2/8. Part of the score of each set of whitetail antlers is composed of four circumference measurements on each antler. The first circumference is taken at the narrowest point between the antler base and the brow tine. The second is between the brow tine and the second point and so on.

The total of all eight circumference measurements from the Lenawee County buck is 55 3/8, according to O'Brien. She said the next highest scoring buck in state records, in terms of mass, is the state record nontypical that Paul Mickey from Kawkawlin shot in Bay County during 1976. The mass of that 29-point rack totals 52 7/8.

Todd Perin is listed in CBM records as the hunter who shot the buck that grew the state's most massive rack. Perin lived in Jasper at the time he tagged the deer, but he was living in Munising during 2004 when he sent me a letter suggesting that his buck should be included in a future edition of Great Michigan Deer Tales due to the exceptional mass of the antlers. He invited me to visit him to see the rack and hear his story and I took him up on the offer.

The fact that Perin owns the deer and legally tagged it, is not in question, nor is the score of the antlers. The controversy is between Perin and a former long time friend of his - Tim Sauter of Palmyra - who shot the buck before Perin did. Sauter thinks they should share credit for the buck. The disagreement about who should get credit for the buck led to the ending of the 22-year friendship between the two. Read on to find out what happened.

When I interviewed Todd, he mentioned Tim's participation in the hunt on which the book buck was taken and the controversy between the two over the deer. I assume he thought I would accept his side of the story as gospel and leave it at that. With my experience as a reporter, however, I realized I had to get the other side of the story, too, so I also interviewed Tim. Both men agree the buck with the exceptional antler mass was taken on a sanctuary of private land that had not been hunted for at least 20 years.

"Three landowners got together and didn't let anybody hunt on their property," Perin said. "There is 17 acres of woods on the property and that's where I got the buck in 1998. What happened is the deer got overpopulated on that sanctuary with no hunting."

A lease agreement was eventually worked out to allow Perin, his brother Shane and Sauter to hunt the sanctuary, with the understanding that they would help reduce the deer population. They took seven does during bow season and waited until the rut to try for one of the trophy bucks living on the sanctuary. Besides the nontypical, which they estimated would score around 150, Perin said there was a 160-class 10-point, two 140 class bucks and a couple of 130s.

"I had the nontypical buck within 17 yards of me one day when I was bowhunting," Todd commented, "but he never cleared the raspberry bushes, so I didn't take a shot."

Opening day of gun season was a Sunday during 1998 and Lenawee County was closed to Sunday hunting at the time, so Perin had to wait until Monday the 16th to hunt with his shotgun. Tim

Sauter said he traveled to an area open to deer hunting on the 15th and shot a nice 8-pointer that scored about 125. On the morning of the 16th, Sauter was hunting from a tree stand about 140 yards from Todd.

"I sat in a ground blind that morning," Perin said. "When you got in a tree in that small woods, they would pick you out. At daylight, I had 28 deer come in. The group included five bucks and a hot doe. For 20 minutes, I had the gun shouldered.

"I was actually trying for the big 10-pointer that morning," Todd stated, "and he was one of those five bucks. Finally, the typical was in the clear on the edge of the woods at 73 yards, but the deer was standing at a bad angle and there was a house in the background, so I didn't take the shot. Then the 10-pointer started fighting with another buck in a field and the hot doe bedded in front of me 40 yards away. I knew the big typical would eventually come to the doe, so I waited.

"When the big buck finally came toward the bedded doe, she stood up and started walking at me, but before the big boy was in position for a shot, I heard shooting behind me. The big typical was gone like the wind."

Sauter was responsible for the shooting that spooked the big typical. The nontypical had come within shotgun range of Tim on the run.

"When the buck got 45 yards away, I aimed behind its right shoulder and shot," Tim said, "and he jumped in the air, but he kept going. I fired at him three more times on a dead run and missed. I hit him again with my fifth shot and flipped him over. The gun was then empty.

"I tried to put another shell in the gun," Sauter continued, "but I couldn't do it before he got up and took off. The buck ran to Todd and I heard him shoot twice. I figured he would finish the deer off for me."

"Soon after I heard the shots behind me is when the heavy-antlered nontypical came running by me 35 yards away," Todd said. "I hit him with my first shot, putting a slug through both shoulders, and missed him with the second. It's a good thing I hit him the first time because my gun jammed after the second shot."

**51**

The whitetail had three holes in it when it went down. Sauter said he was responsible for two on the right side and Perin for one on the left. One of the slugs that entered the right side damaged the buck's liver and the other clipped a lung. Those wounds would have eventually proved fatal, if Todd hadn't shot the deer again.

The fact that Perin made the killing shot on the whitetail, meaning he was the last to shoot it and his slug was responsible for the deer's death, entitled him to tag it, according to Captain Curt Bacon at Marquette, who was the DNR Law Division Supervisor for the UP. He's now retired.

"That's what has evolved as division policy over my 32 year career," Bacon said. "If I'm a referee in a situation over who should tag a deer after it has been shot by more than one person, it's my position that the person who shot it last and put it down has the right to tag it."

That's obviously the position that Perin took in this case. The fact that a trophy buck was involved had a lot to do with Todd's decision. So did the fact that Tim shot a rack buck the day before. On an earlier hunt, Todd finished off a doe that Tim wounded. In that case, Todd let Tim tag the deer.

I know of a number of cases where hunters have shot deer that were wounded by other hunters and the person who killed the whitetail allowed the person who drew first blood to tag it when they followed the blood trail to the carcass. The chapter titled The Barton Buck in this book is an example of that. That's obviously an option, but it's up to the person who finally kills a deer to make that decision. In situations when a trailing hunter doesn't reach a dead deer soon after it's down, it may be too late for that option because hunters are supposed to tag whitetails they shoot as soon as possible.

Even though Perin legally tagged the trophy buck Sauter also shot, Tim feels Todd still could have publicly credited him for his role in the hunt. In fact, the trio knew that at least one of them had an excellent chance of bagging a book buck in the sanctuary and, according to Tim, they had agreed to share the credit if one of them did do that. Shane Perin agrees, but he also said that the other two obviously have different interpretations of what that agreement meant.

Shane tried to get the two to put a higher priority on their friendship than the deer. He thought they would eventually settle their differences and make up. That had not happened when this was written. During conversations with both men, they each sounded regretful about the loss of the friendship they once had.

"I love Todd Perin like he's my brother," Sauter said. "I wish things had turned out differently."

The antler bases are thicker on this Lenawee County buck's antlers than any other whitetail I've ever seen. The first circumference measurement of each antler is 9 inches. The second circumference is 7 3/8 on the right antler and 6 5/8 on the left. The final two circumferences on the right antler are each 6 1/8 inches. Those two measurements on the left antler are 5 6/8 and 5 3/8.

The right beam and one of the tines on the right side are broken. If it weren't for those breaks, the antlers might have netted enough to qualify for national records maintained by the Boone and Crockett Club. They would have at least come close. The B&C minimum for honorable mention of nontypical racks is 185 and it's 195 for alltime listing.

Perin estimated that eight inches of antler was missing from the right beam and six inches had been broken from the tine. A fight with another buck is the suspected cause of the broken antler.

The buck had a dressed weight of 238 pounds. His chest girth was 58 inches and his neck was 33 inches around. He was estimated to be 6 1/2 or 7 1/2 years old.

"The year before I got him, somebody put a broadhead in his left shoulder," Todd said. "That injury affected his antler growth during 1998."

Todd has one of the buck's shed antlers from 1997.

Todd's side of the story was originally published in the April 4, 1999 edition of The Daily Telegram Newspaper, which is published in Adrian. Tim's side of the story was published in the April 11th edition of the newspaper. Both men claim parts of each other's story is inaccurate.

As Perin requested, the story behind the buck that grew the state's most massive antlers is now in an edition of Great Michigan Deer Tales. I suspect the finished product turned out differently than he would have liked. The last time I spoke to him, he said he was moving from Munising back to the southern part of the state.

*Head mount of the Ralph Hobbs buck that he shot in Delta County during 1929. With a net score of 237, the rack would be Michigan's number 2 nontypical.*

# Chapter 7

# *Michigan's Number 2 Nontypical*

A 21-point rack grown by a buck that was shot in the Upper Peninsula's Delta County during November of 1929, which wasn't measured until many years later (2004), would now rank as the state's second highest scoring nontypical. However, there's little doubt the antlers would have outscored the current state record if they had been measured years ago. The rack had shrunk considerably over the 74 years since the deer was shot and the rack was measured.

A portion of the last chapter of Book 2 of Great Michigan Deer Tales is devoted to this buck. At the time that book was published, no information was available about exactly what the antlers scored. Those details are now known. This chapter represents a more complete story behind this outstanding buck.

The antlers have a net score of 237, according to taxidermist Terry Vining from White Cloud, who measured them while he had the rack in his possession to make replicas. The antlers have a 12-point typical frame and nine nontypical points that total 51 6/8 inches in length.

Michigan's current state record nontypical is a 29-pointer that Paul Mickey shot in Bay County during 1976. The monster rack measured 238 2/8, just 1 2/8 inches more than the recent scoring of the big nontypical bagged in 1929. The 21-pointer from 1929 easily shrunk more than 1 2/8 inches between the time the deer was shot and its antlers were measured.

The late Ralph Hobbs is the hunter who shot the enormous nontypical in 1929. He lived near the community of Trenary. A black and white photograph of Hobbs with his exceptional buck was on display in a trophy case at the Negaunee Rod and Gun Club for many years. The club is about 40 miles from Trenary.

The hunter's name and the year are hand written on the photograph along with details about the buck. Those notations put the whitetail's weight at 275 pounds when it was shot. The antlers reportedly had 28 points and the spread between the beams was listed as 31 inches. Based on the length of tines, the number of points, beam lengths and the antler spread, it was obvious the rack would easily surpass the Boone and Crockett minimum of 195 for nontypical antlers.

One of the trustees of the rod and gun club where the photo of Hobbs and his buck was on display decided to try to learn more about the hunter and the deer in 1992. Frank Zeits primarily wanted to find out what happened to the large set of antlers and what they scored. The only details any surviving member of the club knew was limited to what was written on the photo.

One of the people Zeits located who was familiar with Ralph Hobbs and his buck was Hobbs' sister. Her married name was Blanche Furdon and she lived in the small community of Rock near the border of Marquette and Delta Counties. She was 74 years old at the time and had been 13 when her brother bagged the super buck. Bill Shepley from Shingleton, one of Hobbs' nephews, also provided some information. He was 14 years old in the fall of 1929.

According to the facts gathered from people Zeits spoke to, the Hobbs' homestead was four to five miles south of Trenary near railroad tracks east of U.S. Highway 41. The homestead, part of which is visible in the background of the photo of Hobbs with the buck, was in north Delta County. Ralph reportedly shot the enormous whitetail in a swamp about 300 yards from the house while sneak hunting with a .30-30 caliber rifle. Shepley said he helped Hobbs drag the buck from the swamp to the railroad tracks where they loaded it on a push cart.

Ralph Samuelson from Chatham said his father saw the trophy buck cross the highway headed toward Hobbs' home the day before they heard about Hobbs bagging the deer. Samuelson was 17 at the time and remembers the circumstances surrounding the deer well.

Interestingly, 1929 was the first year for what has become Michigan's traditional firearms deer season from November 15-30. During the 16 years prior to 1929, the dates for deer season in the state were November 10-30.

No one could recall exactly what day Hobbs shot the buck, but it was thought to have been after opening day of the season when there was snow on the ground. The black and white picture of him with the deer shows snow on the ground, which is common any time during gun season in the UP. However, there was no snow on the ground on November 15 that year, according to newspapers, and the first decent snowfall didn't arrive until late November.

According to DNR records, there were 68,011 resident deer licenses sold in Michigan during 1929 and 356 nonresident tags, a far cry from the hundreds of thousands of firearm deer licenses sold during recent seasons.

Hobbs' sister told Zeits that her brother traded the big buck for a pair of does and $50. Furdon said two men from Kalamazoo who owned a bar made the trade to get the big whitetail.

When Ralph Hobbs shot the one-of-a-kind buck, meat and money were far more important than antlers. Fifty dollars was a lot of money in those days. And the meat from a pair of does would be tastier than the venison from what could have been a tough old buck.

Zeits was told that Hobbs never married and lived with his mother most of his life. Ralph's mother reportedly didn't have any teeth when he shot the big buck. Under those circumstances, it would have been easier for her to eat the normally tender meat from does.

Hobbs was reportedly in his 30s at the time he shot the world class nontypical and he died in his 60s. He spent a lot of time at a bar in Trenary near where he lived. A photo of him with the big buck was on display in the bar until it was moved to the Negaunee Rod and Gun Club.

It wasn't known what happened to the antlers of the Hobbs Buck until 1998. Brian Denisty from Caledonia owned the rack at the time and it had been in his basement for at least 25 years. Denisty's friend, John Vrona, brought the world class antlers to the attention of Dennis Schmidt, who was the editor of Michigan Sportsman Magazine at the time, and he assigned me the task of digging up the story behind the deer. After getting a polaroid photo of the mounted head from Vrona, I recognized the rack as the one taken by Ralph Hobbs.

Vrona had the rack rough scored at 229 6/8, but that measurement appears to have been inaccurate because the antlers were only credited with 18 scorable points (those at least an inch in length) at that time. Vining came up with 21 points and that would explain the higher score. At least seven of the 28 points the rack was credited with on the old photograph were less than an inch in length by the time they were measured.

It's obvious the antlers would have shrunk more than an inch since the deer was shot, taking into account the 31-inch spread it was credited with in 1929. That was probably the outside spread. That measurement is now 28 7/8 inches. The inside spread is 25 4/8, which is still wider than most whitetails.

As mentioned earlier, the nine nontypical tines total 51 6/8 inches in length. The distinctive pair of drop tines off the right antler and another drop tine on the left antler make it easy to identify this rack. The drops on the right are 12 1/8 and 11 inches long and the one on the right is 9 5/8 inches.

The G2 and 3 typical tines on the right beam are also 12 1/8 and 11 inches long. The third tine on the left side is the longest at 10 2/8 inches. The right beam is shorter than the left at 24 4/8 versus 26 7/8 respectively.

The antlers also have a lot of mass. The beams are 6 1/8 and 6 inches in circumference at the bases. The last circumference measurement is 5 1/8 inches on each side. The antlers have a total of 8 2/8 inches of deductions for symmetry, so the gross score would be 245 2/8.

Something else new known about this buck besides what the antlers score is its age. The skull was used in the original mount and Vining was able to determine the buck was 7 1/2 years old when it was shot by Ralph Hobbs, based on tooth wear. Vining also told me he isn't sure who now owns the original antlers. He said he heard Denisty sold the rack.

A replica of the Hobbs Buck can be seen at the Michigan Whitetail Hall of Fame Museum, which is visible along I-94 east of Jackson. As far as I know, the antlers from this buck have still not been entered into state records.

*Ralph Hobbs with Michigan's number 2 nontypical that he shot in 1929.*

*Photo courtesy Gene Osantowski*

*Gene Osantowski with the Cheboygan County 20-pointer netting 190 4/8 that he got in 2001.*

## Chapter 8

# Northern Lower Peninsula Trophies

Most of the bucks with the biggest antlers in Michigan have been bagged in either the Upper Peninsula or the southern one third of the state, but southern counties have practically had a monopoly on Michigan's largest racks for close to 20 years. There have been some bragging size whitetails tagged in the northern Lower Peninsula all along, too, though. The purpose of this chapter is to provide the stories behind some of them.

During the fall of 2001, for example, the highest scoring nontypical taken during firearms season that was entered in state records for the year was bagged by Gene Osantowski from Cheboygan in Cheboygan County on November 28. The 20-pointer ended up with a final official net tally of 190 4/8, according to state record keeper Commemorative Bucks of Michigan (CBM).

The Osantowski buck ranks third among nontypicals for Cheboygan County. A pair of bucks that qualify for alltime listing in national records maintained by the Boone and Crockett Club (minimum of 195) were taken from the county in the past. Maurice Fullerton bagged a 21-pointer during 1943 that netted 198 4/8 and Richard Campbell shot an 18-pointer that measured 195 7/8 within the borders of the county during 1970, according to CBM.

Also worthy of note is that another nontypical that Gene shot in 1995 from the same spot where he got his buck during 2001, is the fifth highest scoring nontypical for the county. It is a 17-pointer that scores 181 2/8. Osantowski said he got that buck on the last day of

**61**

the December muzzleloader season that year, just before dark. He hadn't seen that deer before he got it.

Gene said there is a possibility that he almost saw the big nontypical he got during 2001 on the very last day of the 2000 black powder deer season. As it was getting dark, he had nice 8 and 10-point bucks in front of him. He commented that they were acting nervous like a bigger whitetail was nearby, but no other buck appeared. After having taken the 20-pointer and knowing it was probably in the area the year before, is how he came to the above conclusion.

The experienced deer hunter passed up the rack bucks that were in front of him on the last day of muzzleloader season because he had filled his first tag with a big 8-pointer during firearms season. He shot that buck while walking to his blind about 2:45 p.m. He let the 10-point go a number of times besides the end of the black powder hunt because it had short tines.

Osantowski did see the nontypical he got toward the end of the 2001 gun hunt on one other occasion before he shot it. That first sighting is what prompted him to hold out for that deer. The 20-pointer has the largest set of antlers of any whitetail he's taken during his long deer hunting career.

Gene said he started deer hunting when he was 14 years old and he was 65 when he got his best buck, so he had been hunting whitetails for 51 years at the time.

"I enjoy deer hunting more now than I used to," Osantowski said. "I have more time to hunt, I know what I'm doing and I have a good spot where I know I'm going to see deer. I enjoy watching deer and understand their behavior, so I don't have to kill one to get something out of hunting."

He commented that he usually manages to tag one buck every year, but he's taken two some years. Like many experienced deer hunters, he's become selective about the bucks he shoots. In fact, he's almost become too selective.

"I almost didn't kill that big nontypical last fall when I had the chance," Osantowski told me when I talked to him in 2002. "I accomplished what I wanted to when I was in position for a shot at him."

Most hunters would have been inclined to shoot at the buck under the circumstances Gene first saw it. However, he spent so much time trying to judge the whitetail that it walked off. He said he probably wouldn't have tried a shot even if he knew how big the buck was right away due to the distance involved.

It was November 15, 2001, opening day of firearms season, when Gene first saw the deer. His wife was in his blind with him that day. It was 4:15 p.m. when the buck appeared.

"He came walking out of the brush about 100 yards away," Osantowski said. "I put the binoculars on this big deer and I couldn't make out exactly what he was, except he was a helluva buck. He was moving his head up and down like he was scenting me.

"I thought I saw antler beams. I told my wife, 'I think there is 6 inches on each side of his ears.' He turned his head sideways and I saw a long tine, then he was gone. That's when I decided to hunt for that deer."

The spot Gene was hunting is on the edge of thick bedding cover that whitetails in his area routinely use. The location has been good to him. He has taken at least one good buck a year from the stand over the 10 years he had been hunting it. He added that he's probably taken other bucks besides the two nontypicals that qualify for entry in state records, but he hasn't had any other antlers measured.

"I scouted that area 10 years ago and I never entered their domain again," Gene said. "I just wait 'em out."

Osantowski stumbled upon the area where he got the book bucks while tracking a wounded deer. All of the beds he encountered in a small area attracted his attention and that's what prompted him to scout the location more thoroughly. His blind overlooks the intersection of a pair of old logging roads surrounded by thick young aspens. There are some pines along a creek bottom to his right where a lot of the deer he sees come from.

After seeing the big buck, Osantowski bought two types of cover scent and Indian Buck Lure that he thought would be attractive to the rutting whitetail and put it out on cotton balls within view of his stand every day he hunted. He saw no indication that the scent made any difference, however. He saw some smaller antlered whitetails such a spikes and forks, but not the one he wanted. The biggest buck he passed up while waiting for the trophy was a 6-pointer.

The season was winding down by the time he finally saw the exceptional buck again. He was in the same blind where he originally spotted the whitetail on the morning of November 28. There was three inches of fresh snow on the ground.

"All of a sudden, at 8:30 a.m., out walked this monster in brush 15 yards in front of me," Gene commented. "At that point, I was really shook up. He came that close and looked right at me. I'm left handed and I couldn't shoot. I thought, 'I'm just going to wait him out.' The look in his eye was that he realized he really messed up.

"He turned sideways and took three steps. Then I was able to get his head in my scope. I knew I would be able to shoot when he took one more step. When he took that step, I touched her off.

"He went out of there like he wasn't hurt," Gene continued. "The day before, I fell and I wondered if I knocked my scope off. If there hadn't been snow, it would have been tough to find him. The buck went 200 yards.

"I later found a big bed 60 yards from where I was sitting that morning in really thick cover. I think that was the bed of the buck I shot. He just came walking out of that thick stuff."

Gene shot his buck with a 180 grain bullet out of a .30-06. The scope he had on the rifle was a 3x-9x variable that he had set on 4 power. The buck weighed 225 pounds in the round and was aged at 5 1/2 years old. When the deer's antlers were green scored, they had a 21-inch inside spread. The beams were 26 and 27 inches long and two tines were over 11 inches in length.

## Otsego's Best Typical

Otsego County's number one typical was collected during the 2000 firearms season by Robert Cannon of Mt. Morris on November 23. The 14-pointer netted an even 170, which is the minimum for alltime listing in Boone and Crockett Records, and was taken on public land. There was a foot of snow on the ground when Cannon and his hunting partner got to the Pigeon River Country State Forest and they only saw one doe during the first couple of days of hunting.

They then did some scouting and found a mix of oak and beech trees that had produced a mast crop. There was a lot of deer sign in that area, including some scrapes and rubs. Robert set his buddy up overlooking the buck sign and then went uphill to a large clearcut where he posted for the evening.

The trophy buck appeared at the edge of the clearcut late in the day. A 210-yard shot from a 7 mm magnum dropped the whitetail on the spot. The buck had a dressed weight of 205 pounds.

### Montmorency Bow Buck

During the fall of 2006, the highest scoring nontypical bow kill recorded for the state came from Montmorency County. Larry Chastain from Holly arrowed the 14-pointer on November 7 that had a gross nontypical score of 191 4/8 and netted 188. That buck is not only the highest scoring nontypical known taken with bow and arrow in the state that year, it's the number one nontypical on record for Montmorency County.

The previous county record was a 19-pointer scoring 185 that was also taken with archery equipment in 1997. The lucky hunter was Bruce Jenkins.

Chastain said he has a cabin at Hillman that he's been deer hunting out of for 30 years. Although he's taken plenty of other whitetails in the county, the buck he got in 2006 is by far his best.

*Photo courtesy Larry Chastain*

*Larry Chastain got this 14-pointer that scored 188 with bow and arrow near Hillman in Montmorency County on November 7, 2006.*

"I got the deer in an area where there were always scrapes, but I never hunted it a lot," Larry commented. "During 2005, I got an 8-point November 4th on the same trail that the bigger buck was using. The 8-point was following a doe.

"A couple of days before I got the big one, I made a couple of mock scrapes, using Buck Fever Synthetic scents."

Chastain said he used a Buckshot climbing tree stand to position himself 18 feet from the ground in a large aspen tree where he could watch the mock scrapes. Some branches from a nearby pine tree provided some cover to breakup his outline. He also sat facing the tree, so the tree trunk itself would prevent deer from seeing him.

A couple of does had been milling around near Larry's stand when the buck finally appeared late in the day.

"When I seen that deer, I knew it was a once in a lifetime buck," he said. "He stopped at 18 yards in a perfect position for a bow shot. I don't mind telling you I had a case of buck fever."

Due to the low light level, Larry wasn't able to follow the flight of his arrow and see where it hit, but he was confident his arrow connected. After the bowhunter climbed out of his stand, he went to get a couple of buddies to help in the recovery effort. When they returned, they located the blood trail and started following it, but they eventually lost it.

They decided to return in the morning and were heading out of the woods when they stumbled upon the dead buck. Coyotes found the deer before they did and had eaten some meat from the hindquarters. Larry didn't have the deer aged, but it had a dressed weight of 180 pounds. He said they figured it would have weighed 10 to 20 pounds heavier if it weren't for the coyotes.

Chastain shot the buck with a 62 pound pull Hoyt bow. He was using carbon express arrows tipped with Tight Point Shuttle T-lock broadheads.

Larry said his best buck with bow and arrow before that fall was a 9-point he got in 1980. He won a contest with that deer and got a free head mount, but he never had the antlers measured on it. He's been bowhunting for about 40 years.

His father introduced him to bowhunting before the days of compound bows. He said he hunted with bow and arrow for a number of years before getting his first whitetail with an arrow. That first bow kill was a spikehorn.

He said he missed the deer with an arrow. It ran a short distance and then returned, not sure about what happened. Larry's second arrow didn't miss.

### Mason County Record

Brad McClure from Custer, who was 18 years old at the time, bagged an impressive 10-pointer on October 14, 2006 in Mason County that netted 161 5/8. The buck is not only a whopper anywhere in the state, it's a county record.

The McClure Buck is the highest scoring typical known taken from the county by any means, according to state records maintained by Commemorative Bucks of Michigan (CBM). The previous number one typical from that county is another 10-point taken by Carl Stevenson during gun season way back in 1925. The antlers on that deer netted 157 7/8.

The day Brad arrowed his record buck was not the first time he had seen the whitetail. He and his family had watched the deer all summer. When its antler development was complete, they guessed that its antlers would score in the 160s and they proved correct.

McClure came close to getting a shot at the impressive whitetail on opening day of bow season. He approached the tree stand Brad was in with two other bucks that had smaller antlers.

"When he was 10 yards away, he looked up at me and blew the whistle," McClure said.

Although the deer saw Brad and knew something was up, it didn't act terribly alarmed when it left the area, so the bowhunter thought he might get another chance at the deer, and he was right. Two weeks later, McClure was in the same stand when an 8-point came uphill into view with the bigger buck trailing behind. Their line of travel would keep them out of bow range, so Brad blew his grunt call to try to lure the whitetail toward him, and it worked.

"The buck got to the same place where he busted me on opening day," McClure said. "This time, there was an opossum nearby that distracted the deer, so I could take the shot."

The whitetail had a dressed weight of 155 pounds and was aged at 3 1/2.

Photo by Richard P. Smith

*Dave Walther with the 19-point nontypical netting 191 2/8*
*that he got in 1990. The buck was 8 1/2 years old.*

## Chapter 9

# *Alger County Trophies*

Alger County has produced its share of monster bucks over the years. Included among those is the highest scoring nontypical recorded in modern times that Dave Walther from AuTrain tagged in 1990. Mark Whitmarsh from Chatham shot a whopper typical in 1991 and Jim Hannah from Shingleton got a nontypical with bow and arrow in 1994 that is the highest scoring nontypical among bow kills for the county.

The Walther Buck ranks third among nontypicals on record for Alger County, but the pair of higher scoring bucks were bagged in 1934 and 1948 respectively. Dr. Karl Beck is credited with the county's best nontypical in state records maintained by Commemorative Bucks of Michigan (CBM), a 22-pointer that netted 212 5/8. A. C. Hamilton collected a 20-pointer that scored 195 6/8.

Dave's buck is an impressive 19-pointer with three long drop tines, one of which is club shaped, that he shot on November 18, 1990. The antlers have an official net score of 191 2/8. If it weren't for the loss of a fourth drop tine that appeared to have been broken off recently when Walther got the whitetail, his deer probably would be in second place for the county. That missing tine would have been more than five inches long. The trio of drop tines that remain are all much longer than that.

By the afternoon of the third day of gun season in 1990, Dave had not yet seen a deer. He found a large scrape about 300 yards from his blind, along the edge of the swamp. To increase his chances of success that day, Walther decided to leave a trail of doe in heat scent from the scrape to his blind.

"When I went to the scrape, it looked like maybe it had been reworked," Dave said. "So I took the doe in heat scent and put it in the scrape. Then I had a 10-inch piece of cloth, which was about an inch wide, that I soaked in the doe in heat scent also. I tied it to my boot and walked to my blind. When I reached my blind, I took the rag off my shoe and tied it onto a limb. Then I commenced to wait."

Walther actually hung the drag rag from a tree about 40 yards from his blind, where he hoped to get a shot at a buck. He didn't put the rag next to the blind.

"I was sitting there for about two hours and just finished reading a magazine," Dave continued, "when I looked out the window of the blind and I seen horns. I said, 'Oh my God!'"

The buck was coming from the opposite direction than Walther had left the scent trail. The whitetail may have been on his way to the scrape, but it smelled the drag rag and was drawn to it, coming within 35 yards of Dave's blind to check out the enticing aroma. It was 4:55 p.m. when the buck was lured to the scent.

"I wanted to drop it with one shot, so I didn't have to go looking for it," Walther said. "I wanted to shoot it in the front shoulder, but there was about a 6-inch tree in the way of the front shoulder. So I was trying to decide between shooting it high in the neck or the ribs for a lung shot.

"I'm going back and forth from neck to ribs, trying to make up my mind what to do. It probably only took me half a second to decide, but it seemed like forever. I finally decided to shoot it in the ribs. I hugged the tree with my crosshairs and touched it off.

"The deer jumped back. It looked like it was going to go down, but it didn't. It just folded a little bit and then took off running. After I pulled the trigger, I was so shook up, I couldn't even...

"My heart was going 90 miles an hour. How do you keep your composure? It was the most exciting two minutes, maybe three minutes, of my life. I honestly thought I was going to have a heart attack!"

Most deer hunters probably understand how Dave was feeling when he shot his trophy buck. Fortunately, he didn't have a heart attack and the 180 grain bullet from his .30-06 did clear the tree to make a killing shot on the buck. With the help of relatives, Walther found the trophy animal 100 yards away.

The lucky hunter said he thought the buck had 10 or 12 points with one drop tine, when he shot it. He was in for an eye opener when he reached the fallen animal. There was no ground shrinkage in this case. The rack was much bigger than expected. As stated previously, the antlers contained three long drop tines. The drop tine that had broken off was on the same side as the pair that were remaining. It had been between those that were still intact.

Walther said his buck proved to be 8 1/2 years old, far older than most bucks bagged in the state, and it had a dressed weight of 206 pounds. The UP is the only region in the state where some antlered whitetails reach that age on a regular basis. Few bucks make it beyond 5 1/2 in the Lower Peninsula.

Dave had been deer hunting for about a dozen years before bagging his drop tine buck. His best buck prior to 1990 was a dandy 8-pointer with an 18-inch spread that had a dressed weight of 250 pounds. He shot the 8-point in 1981 and he said the antlers wouldn't score very high because some of the tines were broken.

Since 1990, Walther has claimed a pair of 8s and a nice 10-pointer that would score in the 130s. He got the 10 on opening morning of the 2005 gun season while hunting over bait.

### The Whitmarsh Buck

Mark Whitmarsh got his trophy typical 10-pointer that grossed 171 1/8 and nets 169 in Alger County on November 22, 1991. He was walking along a big ridge at noon on a farm where he has permission to hunt when their paths crossed. Mark said he knew there was at least one big buck on the farm because he had seen it himself five days earlier and the land owner had seen it that very morning when rounding up his cows. When Whitmarsh shot the whitetail that day, however, he had no idea at the time that it was as big as it proved to be.

Mark was posted where he could see the edge of a large field one evening when he first saw the book buck. Even though the whitetail was a long distance away, he said he didn't have any trouble seeing its antlers. In fact, he watched the deer work a licking branch on a mature balsam fir tree above a scrape along the edge of the field. He said the buck's antlers were easy to see as it moved its elevated head back and forth, with its back to Mark.

Whitmarsh said he later determined the buck was about 200 yards away when he saw it along the edge of the field, but, at the time, he thought the distance was greater than that. Nonetheless, being able to easily see antlers on the head of a whitetail at that distance without the aid of binoculars is an indication they are much bigger than normal. Before the buck was in a position where Mark would have considered taking a shot, it entered the woods and was gone. The spot where Whitmarsh saw the whitetail that evening was about a mile from the ridge where he eventually shot it.

On the morning of November 22, Mark went to a baited blind he had in a different area than the farm where he had seen the big buck. When he hadn't seen anything from the blind by 10:00 a.m., he headed for the farm. There were plenty of other deer on the farm besides the big one, but the sight of the impressive whitetail days earlier along the edge of the field was in the back of his mind.

Mark talked to the land owner when he arrived at the farm and their conversation brought the big buck back to the forefront. The property owner told Whitmarsh he had seen the giant that morning while rounding up his cattle before daylight. The buck stood on the edge of a field while the farmer counted all of the points on its antlers. The farmer told Mark that was the only buck he had ever seen that had long enough points that he was able to count all of them.

The veteran hunter had no idea where the buck would be by then. He made a decision to walk the big ridge due to the fact there were some scrapes along it and the wind was favorable. And that ridge was only about a quarter of a mile from where the buck had been seen by the land owner that morning.

"I only went about 100 yards on the ridge after I climbed it when I saw a doe cross the ridge from right to left," Mark said. "He came along behind her with his head down. I didn't hear him coming or nothing. He just appeared.

"He was only about 20 yards away. I saw he had a rack, so I raised my rifle and shot him, aiming for the neck."

Photo by Richard P. Smith

*Mark Whitmarsh with an impressive 10-pointer scoring 169 that he got with a .223 caliber rifle.*

The whitetail dropped right away and slid down the ridge, so Mark hustled up to where it was right away and shot it a second time in the neck to make sure it was down for keeps. There was good reason for an insurance shot because Whitmarsh was hunting with a light caliber rifle not normally associated with Michigan whitetail hunting. He shot the buck with a .223, which was loaded with 64 grain bullets.

"You can't shoot a deer behind the shoulder with that gun," Mark said, "the bullet is traveling so fast it would pass straight through without opening. I've shot a number of other deer with it. It's real accurate."

When Whitmarsh got a good look at the full dimensions of the downed buck's rack, he was amazed. It didn't take long for him to realize it was the buck he had seen earlier in the season and that the land owner had seen that morning. The farmer got a much closer look at the rack that day when Mark stopped by to show him what he had gotten.

The antlers are more symmetrical than most. They aren't mirror images of one another, but they are close. There's only 2 1/8 inches of differences between measurements on the right and left beams. The biggest difference is in the beam lengths. The right antler is 26 5/8 inches long and the left is 27 4/8, a difference of 7/8-of-an-inch. There's also a half-inch difference in the length of the third tines on each side and a 3/8-inch difference in brow tine lengths.

The second and third tines on each antler have exceptional length. On the right antler, they measured 11 5/8 and 12 inches. Both of those tines were 11 4/8 inches long on the left antler. In sharp contrast to the other points, the brow tines were only about three inches long. Inside spread between the beams taped 18 6/8 inches.

Word spread fast about the whitetail Whitmarsh got. Lots of people stopped by his house to see it. Some of them told him they had seen the deer and they had been trying to get it. One other hunter had even video taped the buck in one of the farmer's fields bordering a road.

Based on the comments Mark heard from other hunters, he determined that the buck had been roaming over about a three mile area. No one else reported getting a shot at the buck though. The whitetail was 5 1/2 years old and had a dressed weight of 193 pounds.

The deer's antlers were far bigger than any others to Mark's credit, but he had taken a big 8-pointer during 1985 that was heavier. The antlers on that 8-point were his biggest until 1991. The rack scored 138 and the deer had a dressed weight of 203 pounds.

Whitmarsh got the big 8 while hunting over bait from a blind one evening. Some does were feeding at the bait when the buck appeared. It hung back on the edge of cover for a while, watching the does. The whitetail's curiosity about the does eventually got the best of him and he approached the bait, giving Mark a shot.

The oldest buck Whitmarsh has taken in Alger County was 9 1/2 years old and he got it in 1993. In spite of its age, that whitetail had a smaller rack and body than his 10-pointer from 1991. Mark's daughter, Megan, turned 14 in 1993, so it was her first year of deer hunting. The pair hunted together from the same blind on opening day of firearms season.

Megan didn't have to wait long to bag her first buck. At 9:30 a.m., she plugged a 2 1/2-year-old 7-pointer with a .243 Sako at a distance of 75 yards. Mark dropped the old timer at 3:45 p.m. with a Winchester .243 at a distance of 100 yards. So the Whitmarshes enjoyed an excellent day of deer hunting!

The 9-year-old buck had a 9-point rack with short tines, including a 2-inch drop tine. The beams were also short, but they were heavy. The buck had a dressed weight of 180 pounds.

Since 1993, Mark said he's seen a couple of other big bucks, including one with a wider rack than his 10-point from 1991, but the tines weren't as long on that one. He wasn't able to tag either buck.

### Hanna Buck

James Hannah from Shingleton bagged a big buck with bow and arrow in Alger County on the evening of October 18, 1993 that had an interesting history. The 16-pointer had a nontypical rack that had an official score of 166 5/8.

Due to a broken tine, Hannah's buck didn't score as high as it could have. The deer slammed into a tree after it was shot, cracking the tine. The point was more than an inch long, but ended up less than an inch in length after it was broken. Tines must be at least an

*Photo by Richard P. Smith*

*Mark Whitmarsh with his oldest Alger County buck that he got in 1993.
It was 9 1/2 years old.*

inch long to be counted as a point.

Besides the broken tine, the antlers had three other projections that were less than an inch in length.

Hannah said he had no idea the buck's antlers had so many points when he shot the whitetail about 6:50 p.m. As the deer approached the bait Jim was watching from his tree stand, he thought the whitetail had a nice 6 or 8-point rack. Once he saw the antlers and decided he wanted the deer, he closed his eyes for a while to help control his excitement as the buck moved into position for a shot. Fortunately, the buck didn't decide to leave while Jim had his eyes closed.

Jim heard the deer coming before he saw it. He heard something walking in the leaves, which alerted him to the whitetail's presence. The buck walked to within four feet of the bait Hanna had placed within easy bow range of his stand and stood there for about 10 minutes. It looked all around to check for potential danger before deciding to eat.

Jim drew his bow when the deer put its head down, but then it looked up as though it heard the movement. The whitetail soon put its head back down and that's when Hanna released his arrow. The buck was standing broadside about 20 yards away when Jim released a Beeman carbon arrow from his 80 pound pull Bear Bow that killed the whitetail. The arrow was tipped with a 4-blade Muzzy broadhead that weighed 90 grains.

After the bowhunter reached the fallen buck he was surprised and pleased with the size of its antlers. He was also surprised by tags in the deer's ears. After checking with the DNR, Hannah learned that the whitetail had been released from the Cusino Wildlife Research Station during March.

DNR Deer Researcher John Ozoga said surplus deer were released from the facility's square mile enclosure, where they live under natural conditions, each year to carefully control deer numbers in the enclosure. Twenty whitetails were released during 1993, 10 of each sex, which Ozoga said is about average. He added that the biggest and oldest buck that was released was killed by a car during May. That animal was 5 1/2 or 6 1/2 years old.

The buck Jim tagged was 3 1/2 and had a live weight of 260 pounds. Its dressed weight was 210 pounds. Ozoga said the buck had a live weight of 199 pounds when it was released. The previous fall the deer had typical 10-point antlers, according to Ozoga.

It's interesting that the whitetail grew so many nontypical points a year later. The deer was obviously in great shape. The brow tines are a unique feature about the rack. They are both exceptionally long and the one on the right side is bladed.

The trophy whitetail was Hannah's fourth bow kill during four years of bowhunting. The other deer he bagged with bow and arrow were does. His best buck with firearms at the time was a 4-pointer.

Jim hunted almost every day of bow season that year, starting on October 1, until getting the trophy nontypical. His persistence obviously paid off. He passed up a couple of small does before the 18th.

More than double the normal number of whitetails from the research facility were released during 1994 due to Ozoga's retirement from the DNR because there are no future plans to continue whitetail studies there. As a result, there were even more trophy bucks roaming the UP woods for bowhunters to try for that year. Some of the bucks that were released were bigger and older than the one Hannah got.

It's unknown if any of those deer made it into state records like the one Hannah got. After Ozoga's retirement from the DNR, all deer were removed from the square mile enclosure at Cusino due to suspension of deer research there.

*Photo by Richard P. Smith*

*Jim Hanna with his nontypical bow kill that measured 166 5/8. He bagged the whitetail after it was released from the DNR's Cusino Research Station.*

*Photo by Richard P. Smith*

*Mark Remali with an 11-pointer netting 171 that he got with a peep-sighted .45/70 on November 15, 2002.*

## Chapter 10

# *Houghton County Booners*

The biggest buck known taken in the Upper Peninsula (UP) during the fall of 2002, in terms of antler size, is a monster 11-pointer collected by Mark Remali from Calumet in Houghton County on opening day of firearms season. The huge antlers are large enough to qualify for national records maintained by the Boone and Crockett (B&C) Club. The rack has an official net score of 171, surpassing the minimum requirement for entry of typical antlers of 170 by an inch.

This is the first buck of that caliber from the UP entered into state records maintained by Commemorative Bucks of Michigan (CBM) since 2000. A pair of B&C qualifiers were bagged in the region that year. Both had nontypical antlers. The minimum for entry of nontypical racks in alltime B&C records is 195.

Jake Jackovich from Calumet got a 26-pointer in Keweenaw County on November 20, 2000 that measured 202 3/8 and Pat Abrams from Curtis nailed a 16-point on November 16 that scored 196 2/8. The stories behind both of those bucks can be found in Book 4 of Great Michigan Deer Tales.

It was during the last minutes of shooting light on November 15, 2002 when Remali got his exceptional buck. He was hunting with an iron sighted .45/70 Marlin lever action rifle that day. The rifle was equipped with a tang mounted, folding peep sight instead of the standard rear sight.

Remali commented that he had been deer hunting with a scoped, Ruger M77 rifle the previous few years and hadn't had much success with that gun, so he considered it bad luck. He switched to the peep-sighted .45/70 in an effort to change his luck and it obviously worked.

Mark said he was confident in his ability with the scopeless rifle. He had practiced a lot with it out to 175 yards, shooting five-inch groups with 405 grain bullets at that distance. The only drawback with the rifle is that iron sights are more difficult to see in low light and that's when the buck appeared.

Remali was in a blind when he first saw the deer at a distance of about 100 yards.

"He came in chasing a bunch of does," Mark said. "I could not see a rack until he came into a field with snow on it. It appeared to be a big rack on a small deer.

"I was wondering if I would be able to see my front sight through the peep, so I checked. The hole on the peep sight was too small to see through in the fading light, so I unscrewed a fitting to increase the size of the sight's opening. Then I was able to see good enough to aim properly.

"I just watched the buck at first because he was busy chasing does. He eventually stopped quartering toward me. That's when I shot. He jumped and ran toward the blind. Based on his reaction, I was sure I hit him.

"He stopped at a distance of 25 to 35 yards, looking into the blind. I expected him to collapse any minute. When he didn't, I thought I might have missed, so I shot a second time. He ran a little ways and stopped.

"Then I shot a third time and he didn't show any reaction. It was obvious I missed him that time. He started to walk and then fell over."

Upon examining the fallen whitetail, Mark confirmed that his first shot did indeed connect. It's a good thing it did. After the first shot, he must have bumped the folding peep sight and it was pulled backward, causing him to miss with the second and third rounds.

When Mark walked up to the fallen buck, he was impressed by the size of its antlers. The rack was so wide, the uppermost beam stuck up high above the ground. The buck's body also looked bigger than it had when he shot it.

Knowing he would need help to handle the carcass, Remali went back to camp. He was warming his hands over the stove when his brother arrived and asked him if he had done any good. When Mark told his brother he got a decent buck, his sibling was anxious to see it and said, "Come on. Let's go get it."

"Not yet. We're going to need one more guy," Mark replied.

That response generated even more curiosity. At first, Mark's brother thought he might be kidding around. That changed when they finally retrieved the whitetail. Bodywise, the buck was not small after all. It had a dressed weight just shy of 220 pounds.

Although Mark had never seen the big buck before the day he shot it, a relative of his had told him about seeing a big 11-pointer earlier in the fall not far from where he shot the deer. He may have gotten the same deer, but he's not sure. The rack has a typical 10-point frame and a sticker on the left brow tine. Tine length of the antlers is exceptional.

The fall of 2002 was Mark's 22nd year of deer hunting. Over those years, he has taken a couple of other trophy bucks. He got another big bodied whitetail within a quarter mile of where he scored in 2002 during 1999, for example. That deer had a nontypical 11-point rack and a dressed weight of 220 pounds.

In 1986 he got another whopper in Ontonagon County that weighed 212 pounds after it was frozen for a week. That buck had a 13-point rack. The antlers from at least one of those bucks should also qualify for state records and Mark might have them measured in the future.

Since 2002, Mark has taken a couple of nice bucks that were at least 3 1/2 years old, but their antlers are much smaller than his best whitetail.

### Beginner's Luck

Inexperienced deer hunters routinely bag some of the highest scoring bucks taken in the state each year and 1990 was no exception. On opening day of firearms season that year Robert Marr from Calumet bagged his first whitetail ever in Houghton County. It was a 15-point nontypical that nets 196 3/8.

Marr didn't get the B&C qualifier during his first year of deer hunting though. It was his second year of serious whitetail hunting when he got the booner. Nonetheless, Robert's first buck was the type most hunters try for their entire lives and many never see.

"I intended to get out hunting at dawn that year," Marr said, "but I had some things to take care of in town that took longer than I expected. I didn't get to the place I planned on hunting until 9:30 a.m. I had a spot in mind where I planned on hunting. It was a ridge overlooking a swamp edge.

"I didn't have a blind. I just planned on standing on the ridge where I had a good view of the swamp. Since it was already daylight when I parked my vehicle, I decided to stillhunt through the woods toward where I planned on standing rather than go directly there. No snow was on the ground."

Robert had only been sneaking through the hardwoods a maximum of 20 minutes when he saw the buck. He shot it at 9:50 a.m. That may very well be one of the shortest hunts on which a Boone and Crockett qualifying buck was bagged.

"He crossed diagonally in front of me," Marr remembered, "and dropped down into a ravine. He was 40 or 50 yards away when I first saw him. His body was already out of sight by the time I got the rifle up. His neck was the only thing still in view, so that's what I aimed for and shot. If I didn't take the shot I had, he was going to be gone in seconds."

Fortunately, Robert's shot connected and the buck dropped. The whitetail was 70 yards away from the hunter when he fired. Robert said he paced the distance off between where he had been standing and where the deer dropped.

The Marlin .45/70 that Marr shot the whitetail with, by the way, was one he borrowed. The rifle was mounted with a 4 power scope. Robert borrowed the gun from his brother-in-law, Brian Keeney.

The beginning deer hunter didn't have any problem telling the buck had antlers when he saw it, but, due to his lack of experience, he had no idea of the rack's dimensions. He didn't have time to dwell on the antlers anyway. He had to get the rifle up as quickly as possible and take the shot.

When Robert reached the fallen buck, he was impressed by its size.

"Oh, wow! That's a big deer," he thought to himself, still not knowing how abnormally large it was. Marr eventually caught on to

*Photo by Richard P. Smith*

*Robert Marr with the head mount of the first deer he ever shot. He got the 15-pointer netting 196 3/8 during his second year of hunting in 1990.*

how exceptional the antlers on his buck were by taking note of the repeated impressive reactions from more experienced hunters who later saw the antlers.

The location where Robert shot the book buck was 200 to 300 yards from where he planned on posting that day. It's a good thing he was late. There was no way Marr could have known it ahead of time, but his timing proved to be excellent. Based on the circumstances, he happened to be in the right place at the right time.

Marr tried to drag the whitetail on the bare ground, but didn't make much, if any, headway. He had to go find a guy he was hunting with who was in the same area, to get help dragging the buck. The deer later had a dressed weight of 234 pounds. No wonder Robert had difficulty trying to drag it himself.

Although most hunters try to be in position by first light, if not before, it's obvious from Marr's example that if you are running late, don't panic. Make the best of it by stillhunting toward your stand. The results could be much better than you imagined.

Robert said he has taken a couple of bucks since 1990, both of which were much smaller. He got a 6-point in 1992 and a 3-point in 1995. Since then, his job has limited the amount of time he has had to hunt, but, no matter how much more he hunts whitetails, the odds of bagging another buck like his first are against him.

### Another Nontypical

On November 21, 2008, veteran deer hunter Bob Vitton from Hancock bagged a huge nontypical 17-pointer in Houghton County that had a gross score of 201 1/8 and netted 195 2/8, according to Commemorative Bucks of Michigan (CBM) measurer Greg Dupuis from Lake Linden. The antlers have a 10-point typical frame, according to Dupuis, and seven nontypical points; three on the right and four on the left. He said total length of the nontypical points came to 28 5/8 inches. Inside spread of the antlers is 18 5/8 inches. Both beams were more than 25 inches in length.

Dupuis said the antlers have a lot of mass. The circumference of both beams at the bases exceeded five inches.

The Vitton buck is one of two B&C qualifiers bagged in the UP during the 2008 firearms deer season and the rack from both deer scored more than any other whitetail entered in state records for the year. This is the first time in many years that UP bucks have taken honors for the largest racks over deer shot in southern Michigan, but, hopefully, it won't be the last time. The second booner was tagged by Bill Rushford from Newberry in Luce County. The 14-point nontypical antlers from the Rushford buck had a gross score of 199 7/8 and netted 197 3/8. The story behind Bill's buck will probably be in Book 6 of this series.

"I've shot many nice deer," Bob Vitton said about his Houghton County buck from 2008. "This one just happens to be the nicest."

Vitton said a neighboring hunter got a trail camera photo of the buck four days before he killed it. The whitetail was seen a number of times during 2007. It reportedly had 15 points then and wider antlers.

"I'm not into big bucks," Vitton admitted, meaning he doesn't specifically hunt for them. If he happens to be lucky enough to get

**86**

one though, as he was in 2008, he doesn't mind. It also means that he didn't enter his deer in state records.

His best buck prior to 2008 had a bigger body, but the antlers were a little smaller. It was a 12-pointer that weighed 210 pounds. Bob said he didn't have the antlers measured on that one.

The 17-pointer had a dressed weight of 185 pounds, but its live weight would have been well over 200. The whitetail was aged at 6 1/2 years old.

"There isn't much to the story about how I got him," Vitton said. "He just walked in and I shot him."

Bob said he was hunting over bait when he got the booner. It was almost 5:00 p.m. when he saw the buck. Other deer were present when the big nontypical showed up. The other deer included some does and a couple of small bucks. One of the bucks was a 6-point.

One shot from Vitton's .30-06 dropped the whitetail in its tracks. He jokingly commented, "Now that I got the big one I can sell all of my guns and retire."

*Photo courtesy Bob Vitton*

***Bob Vitton got this 17-point nontypical on November 21, 2008.
The antlers measured 195 2/8.***

*Photo courtesy Mick LaFountain*

*Mick LaFountain with a 20-point nontypical that he arrowed in Livingston County on October 23, 2000. The antlers scored 209 5/8.*

## Chapter 11

# *Like Winning The Lottery*

Bagging one of Michigan's highest scoring nontypical bow kills during the fall of 2000 was like winning the lottery for Mick La-Fountain from Southfield.

"I'm not the world's greatest bowhunter," he said months later. "I usually hunt with a gun. I've been bowhunting for at least 10 years and I only shot one other deer with bow and arrow. It was a 6-point."

The buck he arrowed in Livingston County on October 23, 2000 was much bigger. The antlers have 10 points per side and a total gross score of 215 6/8. When the 6 1/8 inches of deductions are subtracted, the official net score, according to state record keeper Commemorative Bucks of Michigan (CBM), is 209 5/8.

The rack was the second highest scoring nontypical known taken by a bowhunter in the state at the time Mick shot the deer. A 19-pointer that Paul Kintner bow-bagged in Lenawee County during 1996 was first, with a score of 211. Then, on November 5, 2000, Bruce Heslet II nailed a 23-pointer in Cass County that measured 219 6/8, dropping LaFountain's buck to the third spot, but he doesn't mind.

Since the year Mick bagged his booner, at least two more nontypicals with higher scoring racks have been taken in the state with bow and arrow. One of those is the current state record nontypical bow kill arrowed by Aaron Davis in Hillsdale County. Another chapter in this book is devoted to the hunt for that whitetail.

The 20-pointer Mick got in 2000 still ranks as his best buck and it's going to be tough to collect a bigger one. The LaFountain Deer is the highest scoring nontypical on record for Livingston County, according to the 7th edition of Michigan Big Game Records. One other nontypical of Boone and Crockett proportions has been taken in the county, according to CBM records.

That was also a bow kill. Patrick Harris arrowed the 23-pointer measuring 195 5/8 during December of 1995 and the story behind that buck can be found in Book 2 of Great Michigan Deer Tales.

The county has produced far more booners with typical antlers. A total of six of those are listed in the latest edition of CBM's record book, all but one of which were taken with firearms. They range in score from a 173 4/8-inch 11-pointer that Paul Peckens shot during 1959 to a 180 3/8-inch 15-pointer that Brian Taylor bagged in 1987.

The most recent typical of B&C proportions to come from the county was in 1995. Dolores Kassuba tagged the 12-pointer scoring 174 1/8. The story about her hunt can also be found in Book 2 of Great Michigan Deer Tales.

It was 1992 when Mick bagged his first buck with bow and arrow. He was hunting with a 55 pound pull Lynx Magnum Martin bow, the same one he shot the big nontypical with. The bow is equipped with one sight pin set for 20 yards. He shoots with fingers, having rubber grips on his bow string.

"I was hunting an opening on a powerline on property owned by my brother near Cadillac," LaFountain said. "He suggested I hunt there. I put some carrots down before climbing in a tree.

"Just as it was getting dark, a 6-point came to the carrots I just put out and I shot him. It was a pass through. A double lung shot. I was so happy."

Mick is color blind, so he relied on his brother to follow the blood trail from the 6-point, but it didn't go far.

Prior to '92, LaFountain said he bowhunted on and off for a few years. He was more into hunting whitetails with firearms, frequently traveling to the UP to hunt with a rifle. Two of his best bucks prior to 2000 were taken with a rifle in Iron County near Crystal Falls. One was an 8-point that scored 126 and the other was a 9-point that measured 133.

Both bucks were shot with a Weatherby .257 magnum. He used to hunt with 100 grain bullets, but now uses bullets that weigh 120 grains. The 8-pointer was following a hot doe when Mick shot it. He was posted along some railroad tracks when he got the 9. It stepped out less than 30 yards away.

While hunting in the UP during firearms season, LaFountain said he saw a buck with a typical rack that was larger than the 20-pointer he got during the fall of 2000. It was chasing a doe and it was gone before he could get his gun up. He later shot a smaller buck from a different spot and got turned around, preventing him from getting out of the woods until well after dark.

He went to retrieve the buck he shot the next morning. By then, some one else had taken it.

"I've seen one other buck that would make this one (nontypical bow kill) look like a spike," Mick said. "I saw him in Minnesota when I was in my truck. He took up half the road."

LaFountain saw his high ranking Michigan nontypical once before he got it. It was a week earlier.

"I had been grunting and rattling and he came to check it out," Mick said. "It was getting too dark too fast when he showed up, so I took the arrow off my string as he was walking in. I didn't want to risk making a poor shot.

"He came within 25 yards of me and ground his teeth. He stood there looking right at me for eight to 10 minutes and then walked on by. I had seen an 8-point 20 minutes earlier. The big buck went sniffing after that 8-point when he left.

"I was in awe of seeing something so big. I knew he had a big rack, but not how big. Local farmers had mentioned there were some decent bucks in the area, but they hadn't said anything about a buck like the one I saw."

Mick was in an ash tree when he saw the trophy buck. He was perched on some big limbs in the tree. It was a week later before he could hunt again due to work. He climbed back into that ash tree on the evening of October 23rd.

He carried a Scent Lok Suit with him in a plastic bag until about 50 yards from the tree. When within 50 yards of the tree he planned to hunt from, Mick changed out of his work clothes and into the

Scent Lok Suit. He also emptied his bladder and put fox urine on his boots.

"I let the area settle down for 30 to 40 minutes before grunting with a Rod Benson call," LaFountain said. "Then I did some rattling with a rattle bag. The first buck I saw was an 8-point. He bedded down with a doe about 40 yards away.

"The big buck came in about 20 minutes after I rattled when it was about 5:30 p.m. Branches started popping directly behind me and out he came. He went to town on a bush with his antlers.

"Then he started to circle toward where I put the Scent Lok Suit on and urinated. I knew I had to change the buck's direction, so I began rattling and grunting vigorously," Mick continued. "That caught his attention and he took the same path I had taken to the tree I was in.

"He came right under me and stared up at me for more than five minutes, but it seemed like an eternity. I repeated to myself, 'Don't look at the antlers. Don't look at the antlers.' I stared straight ahead instead of looking down to avoid doing that.

"The buck eventually put his head down and took a few steps away from the tree. Then he stopped and looked back at me again. I remained perfectly still.

"The dominant buck then started raking over another shrub and I knew that was my chance for a shot. He was no more than eight yards away. When I got the bow back, I aimed low to compensate for the close shot. It's a good thing I did because my arrow hit him in the spine.

"He hit the ground like a ton of bricks. I've never seen a deer go down so fast. If I hadn't aimed low, I would have missed the buck of a lifetime."

Mick tried to put a finishing shot in the buck from the tree, but he wasn't able to, so he climbed down and put another arrow behind the buck's shoulder. The antlers have a 10-point typical frame along with five nontypical points per beam. Total length of nontypical points is 44 7/8 inches, with 23 3/8 inches on the right antler and 21 4/8 on the left.

The right and left antlers are 24 4/8 and 25 3/8 inches long respectively. The G2 tines are the longest, with the one on the right measuring 11 inches and the left one taping 10. The left G3 tine is 10 6/8 inches long, but the right G3 is only 9 1/8 inches.

The inside spread between the beams is 21 inches and the base of both antlers are just over five inches in circumference. The buck had an estimated dressed weight of 210 pounds. Taxidermist Mark Freshour of Wallhangers Trophy Taxidermy in Constantine did an excellent mount of LaFountain's buck.

Mick is now a far more experienced bowhunter and has been consistently successful with archery equipment on book bucks during recent years. In fact, he arrowed a pair of book bucks each year during 2007 and 2008. The pair of whitetails from 2007 were especially impressive.

On October 14 that year, he collected a 14-point nontypical that nets 158 2/8. LaFountain nailed another whopper with typical 10-point antlers from the same stand on December 17 that scored 165. Two weeks earlier, Mick grazed the same buck with an arrow when his bow string hit the collar of a new coat he was wearing.

To increase his chances of taking trophy whitetails these days, LaFountain routinely passes up small bucks as well as some that would qualify for record book listing. He reported passing up over 70 bucks during the fall of 2007.

*Photo by Richard P. Smith*

***Mick LaFountain with the head mount of his B&C nontypical bow kill.***

*Photo courtesy Chuck Sullivan*

*Here's Chuck Sullivan with his Boone and Crockett bow kill from Jackson County.*

# Chapter 12

# *Jackson County Bow Bucks*

Jackson County remains one of the best counties in the state for producing big antlered whitetails. The current state record typical came from that county and so have other high ranking typicals. Each previous edition of Great Michigan Deer Tales has featured at least one booner bagged in the county and this one will be no different.

This chapter, in fact, is about two whoppers bagged in the county with bow and arrow. They are the two highest scoring typical bow kills currently listed in state records for the county. Chuck Sullivan from Grass Lake got a 10-pointer on November 4, 2000, scoring 180 1/8, that presently ranks first for the county in the archery category.

Craig Calderone from Grass Lake actually arrowed a 14-pointer in Jackson County that measured 193 2/8 on November 6, 1986, but, at the present time, it isn't in state records. To find out why, you will have to read Book 1 of Great Michigan Deer Tales.

A 13-pointer that Paul Calvert of Leslie downed with an arrow on November 7, 2003, is also covered in this chapter. It is the second highest scoring typical bow kill for the county currently in state records. With a net score of 178 4/8, the Calvert Buck was the highest scoring typical known taken in Michigan that year.

Chuck Sullivan's 10-pointer was the highest scoring typical bow kill known taken in the state during 2000. It ranked fourth in the state among typical bow kills when this was written in 2009.

Chuck Sullivan decided to bow hunt for whitetails on the morning of November 4, 2000 at the urging of his father, Joe. Chuck had just returned from a hunt in the western U.S. when he got a telephone call from his father on November 3. Joe was all excited about a big buck he had seen and video taped that day. He wanted his son to try for that whitetail, so Chuck was in position before daylight on the next morning he could hunt, which was the 4th.

Little did he realize he would be in for one of the most exciting mornings of bow hunting he had ever experienced. Chuck said he started bow hunting with a recurve bow when he was 12 years old. However, he wasn't successful in taking a deer with that bow and soon lost interest.

Sullivan got back into bow hunting nine years before he got the big one, at the age of 37, when he went to a sporting goods auction and successfully bid on a Bear Whitetail bow. He made his first archery kill with that bow, connecting on a spikehorn. That got him hooked on bow hunting.

"I've given up duck hunting and so many other things because I'm hooked on bow hunting," Chuck said. "I enjoy it so much, I look forward to it every year. I've shot enough deer now that I only shoot bucks with 8-point racks or better. I know that if I don't get a good one with bow and arrow, I can always get a good one during gun season."

Chuck's best buck prior to 2000 was a 10-point that would score around 120. He got it with a shotgun around 1988. That whitetail had a dressed weight of 172 pounds. He had also tagged some respectable 8-points and a 9 with a firearm. His best bow kills prior to 2000 were yearling 8-points with basket racks (4 of them).

"I saw five bucks on October 1, 2000. They were two spikes, two 4-points and a 6-point. I saw three bucks the next day. Then I experienced a 10-day drought when I didn't see any bucks.

"I probably passed up 10 to 12 bucks that year before I went out west. The biggest one was an 8-point that would have scored around 120."

It was that same 8-point that Chuck almost shot on the morning of November 4 while seated in a 16-foot ladder stand secured to an oak tree. The stand was in a bottleneck where two marshes come together on the back side of a 5-acre stand of oaks. The marshes are on the edge of a big swamp. Chuck said he had taken five bucks from that stand over the years, including a 6-point he shot the year before.

It was close to 8:30 a.m. when Sullivan saw the nice 8-point coming out of the marsh. He knew the whitetail was going to pass within easy bow range, so he came to full draw and prepared for a shot. The deer was only 15 yards away when it came out of the marsh, but there was some small brush in the way.

When the buck reached an opening, Chuck whistled to stop it for the shot, but the whitetail didn't react as expected.

"Instead of stopping, the buck scooted ahead," Sullivan said. "So I didn't shoot. He went to a scrape about 40 yards away and I watched him freshen it before he went out of sight."

At the time, Chuck had no idea how lucky he was that the 8-point failed to give him a bow shot. If he would have killed that whitetail, there's an excellent chance he would not have gotten the much bigger buck that morning.

"There was a doe about 60 yards away that was looking in my direction," Sullivan continued. "At first, I thought the doe was looking at me. Then I heard all of this splashing and crashing behind me that is what she must have been focused on. I saw does running in a couple of different directions and then I saw a buck chasing a doe.

"The buck and doe were coming from the direction where the 8-point disappeared, so I thought that was the buck that was after the doe," Chuck continued. "All I saw was a rack. I couldn't tell how big it was. It was natural to assume it was the buck I had just seen.

"The buck was chasing the doe down a trail that came right in front of me at 18 yards. I came to full draw on the trail, so I would be ready for a shot when the buck was in the open. When the doe came into view, I looked back and saw the buck coming at a trot.

"It was like the buck's movements were choreographed just for me. It went from a trot to a walk, giving me a perfect shot at 18 yards. That was great. I made a double lung shot.

"He only went 20 yards and stopped. He was looking around like he was trying to get his bearings. Concerned that he might not be hit as good as I thought, I put a second arrow on the string and shot him again. He went another 20 yards before running into a tree and going down. I saw him go down.

"The rack was so wide, it held his head up. When I got to him, I didn't know what to do next. It was like my first time of getting a buck with bow and arrow. I was so excited.

"I started to go get the tractor to transport him because I knew he was too big for me to drag by myself, but then I didn't want to leave the deer either. I tagged and gutted the deer. By then I was calmed down enough to go get the tractor."

Chuck shot the buck with a 62 pound pull High Country Supreme bow, which has a 2-inch overdraw. He was using Gold Tip carbon arrows and a 100 grain Satellite broadhead. He shoots with a release. Sullivan was wearing a Scent Blocker Suit in Mossy Oak camo.

The buck was aged at 3 1/2 and it had a dressed weight of 196 pounds. Chuck was convinced he had gotten the big buck his father had seen. However, when his father saw the deer, he said it was a

*Photo courtesy Chuck Sullivan*

*Chuck Sullivan shows off the head mount of the monster 10-pointer he got in Jackson County on November 4, 2000 that nets 180 1/8.*

different whitetail. The buck Chuck shot was much bigger than the one his father was so excited about. After looking at his father's video, he realized the deer on the tape was a 10-point that would score about 130.

On November 5, a friend of Chuck's was hunting the same property and he saw still another big 10-pointer. The antlers weren't as wide on that whitetail as the one Chuck shot, but the tines were similar. The longest tines were 12 inches long on Sullivan's buck.

"I knew the buck I got was a great deer," Chuck said, "but I didn't realize what I really had until I brought the head to the taxidermist. He thought it was a booner and he was obviously right."

Sullivan credits his success to the "luck of being in the right place at the right time." Chuck filled his second buck tag with a 2 1/2-year-old 8-pointer during firearms season. Its antlers measured between 105 and 110.

### The Calvert Buck

The year 2003 was the second year in a row that Jackson County produced Michigan's highest scoring typical. In 2002, Brian Kessman connected on the year's best typical with a shotgun on November 15. The 11-pointer netted 182 1/8. The story behind the Kessman buck is in Book 4 of Great Michigan Deer Tales.

The 13-pointer that Paul Calvert arrowed on November 7, 2003 has a gross score of 184 4/8 and nets 178 4/8, according to CBM measurer John Knevel of Parma. The antlers have a 12-point typical frame with a 1 4/8-inch nontypical tine growing from the third point (G3) on the left antler.

On a statewide basis, the Calvert buck currently ranks fifth among typical bow kills behind the 10-pointer taken in the same county by Chuck Sullivan. The fact that bucks as young as 3 1/2 years old in Jackson County are capable of growing world class antlers is why the county produces such whoppers. That's how old Calvert's bucks was. Growing 180 inches of antler at that age is much better than average. It's phenomenal, but that's what happens when there's the right mix of genetics and nutrition.

Paul saw the Boone and Crockett qualifying buck on two occasions before he got him.

"I heard about the buck from some friends of mine in July," Calvert said. "They saw the deer feeding in a field on private property. I have permission to hunt 25 acres near that field. By July, even though his antlers weren't fully developed, it was obvious he was going to have a huge rack.

"I drove by the area at prime time during August and there were 15 to 20 deer in the field. Ten to 12 of them were bucks. Three of the bucks were noticeably bigger than the others. The one I ended up

*Photo courtesy Paul Calvert*

***Paul Calvert with 2003's best typical for the state. The 13-pointer he arrowed on November 7 had an official score of 178 4/8.***

shooting was the biggest.

"The other two big bucks were an 8-point and 10-point. The 8-point was in the 130 to 140-class and the 10-point would probably score in the high 130s. He had a 17-inch spread."

Paul knows what a 130-class buck looks like. Until the fall of 2003, his best buck was an 11-pointer he got with bow and arrow on October 1, 1998. It netted 131 5/8. He shot that whitetail from the same tree stand where he got the booner during 2003.

"The stand is in a finger of trees that extends into a swamp and marsh," Paul said. "It's actually a peninsula. Deer usually travel along the peninsula back and forth between bedding and feeding areas. Some of the trees on the peninsula are oaks, so when there's acorns, they do some feeding there, too."

The stand Calvert shot his two best bucks from is in a maple tree. The hang-on stand is about 20 feet from the ground.

Paul has been bowhunting since 1985 and he usually gets a pair of bucks each year during archery season. He doesn't do much gun hunting for deer because he's normally tagged out by the time the season begins. However, he had taken three bucks with firearms prior to 2003.

The archer has been wearing a Scent Lok Suit since 1998. He said he thinks the scent absorbing clothing reduces the chances of deer detecting his presence. He also wears rubber boots when bow-hunting to reduce the amount of scent he leaves on the ground when walking to and from his stands.

The second time Calvert saw the Boone and Crockett 13-pointer before the day he got it was during the youth deer hunt in late September.

"I snuck in there during the youth hunt with my 16-year-old son," Paul said. "We sat in separate tree stands, so we could see different areas. On Saturday morning, I spotted the big 8-pointer that I saw in the field during August, but my son didn't see it. On Saturday evening, I saw the biggest buck. He knew something wasn't right and didn't come close. My son didn't see him either.

"On Sunday, my son shot a 5-point. He was hunting with a gun."

Paul filled his first buck tag for 2003 on October 27. He arrowed an 8-point on which he estimated the antlers would score between

90 and 100.

"He was limping pretty bad when he came through, so I decided to take him," Calvert told me. "He had a wound high on one shoulder. I thought he had been wounded by another bowhunter."

A telephone call from Paul's boss on November 6th set the stage for Calvert to score on the booner.

"My boss hunted that day and he told me the rut had really kicked in," Calvert said. "He said bucks were chasing does all over. So I made plans to hunt on the 7th. It was real windy that day. As I walked toward my tree stand on the 7th, I saw a bunch of big rubs that hadn't been there before. That got me real fired up.

"I got in my stand at 3:15 p.m. I saw the big buck chasing a doe at 3:20. I watched him chase her around for about a half hour and then they disappeared.

"Then I tried rattling and had a 6-point and a buck with half a rack come in. One of the half rack's antlers had been broken off. I also saw the 10-point with the 17-inch spread following the scent of the doe that the big buck had been chasing.

"Bucks were definitely active," Paul continued. "The 6-pointer ended up practically underneath my tree stand. I took out my grunt tube and was playing around with that to see what kind of reaction I would get out of the small buck.

"About 5:00 p.m. I saw the big buck again. He was approaching a shooting lane at a distance of 35 yards. When he got to the shooting lane, he stopped and looked the other way. He posed for me while I made the shot.

"I didn't get nervous until he ran off and I knew I had made a good shot," Paul commented. "I heard a crash when the buck went down. Five minutes after I heard the buck I shot go down, I heard another crash. Then I saw the half rack buck. I think he was trying to get the big buck to stand up.

"After I shot the big buck, the doe he had been chasing showed up. I think the buck was trying to cut her off when he gave me the shot. That's why he was looking away from me. When I climbed down from my tree stand, the 6-point and half rack were with the doe about 50 yards away."

Paul shot the buck with a 70 pound pull Mathews Featherlite bow and 75/95 Gold Tip arrows. A 100 grain Rocket broadhead was on the end of his arrow.

The whitetail's antlers had excellent beam and tine length. The right beam was 28 6/8 inches long and the left measured 28 4/8 inches. Interestingly, the beam tips are only three inches apart. The second tines (G2s) were the longest at 12 4/8 and 12 5/8 inches. The inside spread between the beams is 19 inches.

The buck's dressed weight is indicative of its young age. The deer only weighed 156 pounds. Even though Chuck Sullivan's buck was also aged at 3 1/2, based on tooth wear, I think it might have been a year older due to its weight. The Sullivan buck had a dressed weight of 196 pounds. Tooth wear varies from area to area, so it's not unusual for that to be off by a year.

*Photo courtesy Paul Calvert*

*A side view of the world class rack grown by the Calvert Buck.*

*Photo courtesy Julie Munting*

*Todd Munting with the 18-pointer he got with bow and arrow in Van Buren County during 2002 that netted 196.*

# Chapter 13

# *Two Nontypicals For The Books*

Most whitetail hunters would be happy to bag one buck with nontypical antlers of record book proportions and Todd Munting from Mattawan is no exception. He accomplished the feat on October 13, 2002, bagging a monster 18-pointer with bow and arrow that grossed 202 1/8 and netted 196, exceeding the minimums for national records maintained by both the Pope and Young and Boone and Crockett Clubs as well as a high-ranking spot in state records among bow kills.

What sets Munting apart from most hunters is he managed to collect a second book buck with nontypical antlers that are large enough to qualify for B&C Records. He got his second booner in 2004, nailing it with a muzzleloader after missing it with an arrow. Ironically, Todd shot his second book nontypical with a muzzleloader that he won as a result of shooting the first one. But before covering the details about his second trophy whitetail, let's look at the one he got in 2002.

That was the second year in a row that one of the best bucks known taken with bow and arrow in Michigan was arrowed in southwest Michigan's Van Buren County. Charles Felcyn from Paw Paw bagged an exceptional 11-pointer with typical antlers on November 5, 2001 that grossed 173 6/8 and netted 167 2/8. Todd's buck came in second place among nontypicals taken with a bow in 2002.

Nontypical bow kills only have to score 125 to make it into state records. The Pope and Young minimum for the same category is 150 and it takes at least 185 inches of nontypical antler to be considered for listing with Boone and Crockett in their honorable mention category. A minimum of 195 is required for nontypical antlers to make B&C's alltime listings.

Munting's buck was the second highest scoring nontypical taken with archery equipment on record for Van Buren County when this was written in 2009. Bob Reitz from Paw Paw arrowed a 20-pointer on October 25, 2007 in the county that nets 206 1/8 and grossed 208 3/8, putting it in first place. A pair of nontypical gun kills from Van Buren County that score more than Munting's are a 29-pointer scoring 199 3/8 that was taken in 1989 by 14-year-old Michael DeRosa and a 20-pointer netting 197 2/8 that John Pierson shot during 2000.

The buck Todd bagged in 2002 was and is his biggest. It was the seventh antlered whitetail to his credit when he got it; the fifth with bow and arrow. At the time, he had taken one buck each with a shotgun and muzzleloader.

A 9-pointer with a 14-inch spread that Munting arrowed three or four years prior to his first nontypical, was his best buck until 2002. He got the 9-point during the evening from a tree stand in a funnel between a pair of cornfields. Munting started bowhunting when he was 14 years old and he was 20 in 2002. Todd said everybody in his family bowhunts, so it was natural for him to also take up bow and arrow to follow their lead.

He credits the arrival of a cold front on October 13 for playing a role in his success on the big nontypical.

"It was real windy during the day," Todd said, "but the wind calmed down during the afternoon about 2:00 p.m. I don't remember how cold it got that day, but it was cooler than normal. The weather had been warm until then."

That afternoon Munting climbed into a hang-on tree stand that was 12 to 15 feet from the ground. The tree stand overlooked a valley that funneled down to a cedar swamp. The valley led uphill to some farmland beyond Todd's stand. That fall was the second year he hunted from that stand.

"I saw quite a few nice bucks from the same stand during 2001," Todd said, "but I never had an opportunity to get one of them. I had bucks within 30 yards of me the year before, but something always seemed to go wrong and I never got a shot. Either I was in the wrong position or they were in the wrong spot.

"The best buck I saw the year before had an 8 or 10-point rack. I don't think any of the bucks I saw were the nontypical I got in 2002. There's usually a lot of antler-rubbed trees in the area where that tree stand is. Some of the rubs were on big trees. That's one of the reasons I hunted there."

October 13th was the third or fourth time Todd had hunted the stand during the 2002 season. He had seen four does the morning before. Earlier he had seen some does, a couple of small bucks and a buck with a scrubby half rack that he passed up.

Munting was hunting with the same bow he had taken his previous bow bucks with, a 75 pound pull PSE with a 70 percent letoff. The bow is equipped with a pair of sight pins, one set for 20 yards and the other for 30. He was using Game Tracker carbon arrows tipped with Thunderhead 100 broadheads. Todd uses a Free Flite release for shooting his bow.

The Boone and Crockett buck appeared suddenly about an hour before dark.

"I was just looking around when, to my right, I saw the head and rack moving," Munting told me. "He was coming toward me, so I stood up and got ready. At 10 yards he stopped and was staring straight at me, so I froze.

"He eventually turned and started walking away. When he was about 20 yards from me, he made a sharp left between some trees and I drew my bow. He was walking when I shot. Because he was walking, I hit him a little farther back than I wanted to, but it still looked like a good hit.

"He sprinted about 30 yards and then stopped and started swaying back and forth," Todd continued. "He stumbled a little further and then went down.

"I knew the buck had a big rack. The rack looked out of proportion to the body. I tried not to concentrate on the rack when I was preparing for a shot. After I made the shot and saw him go down, I thought he was a 12-pointer. I noticed that his tines were real long."

When it was almost dark, Todd climbed out of his tree stand and approached his buck. He thought it would be dead by then. However, it wasn't. When he got close to it, the deer got up and went a short distance before going down again.

Todd wisely backed off and decided to get some help. He eventually called home after failing to reach any of his friends and his mother answered the telephone.

"He was hysterical when he called," Julie Munting said. "He called because he couldn't find anyone to help him drag the deer out of the woods. All of his friends were hunting, too. But he did eventually get ahold of Brad Bell and he called back to tell me that."

Brad was working that night and Todd was able to contact him as soon as he got home from work. Brad is also a bowhunter. He had taken an 8-pointer the weekend before.

The buck was dead by the time Todd and Brad got back to where Todd had last seen it. The arrow had gone through the back of the lungs and that's why it took longer than expected for it to expire. Todd got his first good look at the size of the buck's rack when they reached the fallen deer and it was much bigger than he thought it was.

"At first, I couldn't really believe what I was seeing," Todd said. "I thought my eyes were playing tricks on me. Once we realized how big the rack was, we started jumping around and hollering."

The buck's antlers have 10 points on the right side and 8 on the left. It has a 10-point typical frame with 8 nontypical points (3 on the right and 5 on the left) that total 27 6/8 inches in length. Four of the tines are more than 10 inches in length. The second tine on the right side is the longest at 12 1/8 inches.

Inside spread between the beams is only 16 inches and the beams are only a little over 22 inches in length, but the antlers have a lot of mass. The circumference measurement at the base of the right antler is 6 inches and that measurement is 5 4/8 inches on the left side. The smallest circumferences on both beams is 4 6/8 inches.

The buck also had a big body, weighing 250 pounds dressed. The deer would have had a live weight of around 300 pounds. Its age was estimated at 5 1/2.

## The Second One

Todd was hunting in Kalamazoo County when he got his second big nontypical with a .50 caliber muzzleloader on November 18, 2004 that nets 187 4/8. Although 195 is the minimum for alltime listing in Boone and Crockett Records, nontypicals that measure at least 185 qualify for the honorable mention category and are listed in the records for the scoring period during which they were taken. The rack on the nontypical he got in 2004 has 16 points. Even though the second nontypical was taken in a different county, the locations where the pair of booners were bagged are only about 10 miles apart.

If things had gone a little differently, Todd would have gotten his most recent nontypical with archery equipment, too. He was bowhunting from a tree stand during late October of 2004 when a pair of bucks, one of which was the nontypical, started fighting about 75 yards away. The second buck was a decent 8-pointer.

Munting said the bucks squared off on a 2-track that separated a pair of cornfields. There was a big opening where vehicles often turned around at the spot where the bucks fought. Todd said he watched them go at it for about 45 minutes.

When the fight broke up, Todd used a grunt call to try to lure one of the bucks within bow range. The bigger buck came straight to him in response to the calls, perhaps looking for another fight. When the buck was within 25 yards, Todd prepared to take a shot.

After coming to full draw, Munting said he saw a limb that was in the way of a clear shot, so he ducked down to shoot under it. In the process, he bumped the trigger on his release and his arrow was on its way prematurely, not coming anywhere near the buck. The arrow release spooked the buck and it ran off.

On November 18, Todd was hunting with a .50 caliber Knight muzzleloader that he won from a big buck contest he entered the nontypical in that he got during 2002. The stand he occupied that day was about a quarter mile from where he flubbed the opportunity at the nontypical with an arrow. The tree he was in was on a grassy knoll next to a pond in the middle of a patch of woods. The reason he selected that location to hunt from is the area was tore up with buck sign.

Todd said it was hot and humid that day and he was concerned about working up a sweat getting to his stand, so he dressed as lightly as possible. He brought extra layers with him to put on as the temperature dropped in the evening. He had already put a couple of layers on by the time he heard something coming that sounded big. A short time later, the buck appeared about 50 yards away.

Munting could tell it was a good buck, but he said it looked like an 8-pointer. The whitetail was standing behind a small tree and he decided to take it when it stepped out from behind the tree. Minutes later, when the deer hadn't moved, Todd saw an opening he thought he could get a bullet through and took the shot.

The buck piled up after covering 50 yards. Needless to say, Todd was pleasantly surprised when he discovered the whitetail had twice as many points as he originally thought and was the buck he came close to getting with an arrow.

The rack has a typical 8-point frame, with a total of 9 points on the right beam and 7 on the left. The five nontypical tines on the right antler and three on the left had a total length of 28 2/8 inches. Both brow tines were close to eight inches long and the second tine on each side were more than 12 iches in length.

The antler beams were 24 7/8 (right) and 25 7/8 inches long and the inside spread was 17 6/8 inches. Gross score of the antlers came to 191 7/8 and there were 4 3/8 inches of deductions.

The big nontypical proved to be 4 1/2 years old, according to the DNR, who examined its teeth. Todd said the buck wasn't weighed, but it had a longer body than the nontypical he shot in 2002. Since it was shot later in the fall, however, it had lost more weight during the rut. He estimated its weight at about 200 pounds.

*Photo courtesy Todd Munting*

*Todd got his second trophy nontypical on November 18, 2004 in Kalamazoo County with a muzzleloader he won from the buck he got in 2002. He missed the 16-pointer with an arrow in October.*

*Larry Ridley with Michigan's highest scoring antlered doe.
It could also be a world record. The 15-pointer grosses 181 3/8,
but only nets 165 2/8 due to many deductions.*

# Chapter 14

# *Antlered Doe For The Records*

Larry Ridley from Lansing bagged what he thought was a trophy whitetail buck on Thanksgiving morning during 2002 (November 28) in Van Buren County, but, in reality, it proved to be an antlered doe. A one-of-a-kind antlered doe that had a rack much larger than any other antlered doe known taken in the state. In fact, it could be the highest scoring antlered doe for North America.

The unique deer's 15-point nontypical rack has an amazing Boone and Crockett gross score of 181 3/8 and nets 165 2/8, easily qualifying it for a place in state records. That's a lot of bone. The minimum score of nontypical gun kills for entry into state records maintained by Commemorative Bucks of Michigan (CBM) is 150.

Although the majority of deer entered in CBM records are bucks, there's at least one other antlered doe, according to former CBM spokesperson Tira O'Brien. She said she recalls entering an antlered doe with a typical rack scoring in the 130s that was taken years ago.

The antlered doe was Ridley's second deer during his second year of whitetail hunting. He got a 6-pointer during his first year of hunting. Cousins Jon and Arthur Tippman introduced Larry to deer hunting. They selected locations for him to hunt and loaned him a 12 gauge Benelli pump shotgun to hunt with.

Jon saw the antlered doe on opening weekend of the 2002 fire-arms season, but he had no way of knowing it was a doe. He spotted it across a cut soybean field with binoculars, well beyond shotgun range. The large antlered whitetail was bedded next to a buck with small antlers.

At the time, Jon thought it was strange that a mature buck would tolerate a young buck so close during the peak of the rut, but it would all make sense later.

The only deer Larry saw on opening weekend that year was an antlerless doe. He thought about shooting it and was aiming at the doe when he changed his mind and decided to wait. Larry was unable to hunt again until Thanksgiving morning. There was two inches of fresh snow on the ground that morning and, before daylight, Larry climbed into the same tree stand where he shot the 6-pointer the year before.

The stand overlooked a river. The deer that he thought was a big buck showed up at 8:15 a.m.

"From my right, out of the corner of my eye, I caught movement and turned my head to see the largest antlered buck I ever saw trotting through the trees, barely making a sound," Larry wrote in his account of the hunt. "The deer had been following the river's edge and was going to pass diagonally in front of me, angling further away as he went. Fortunately, the Benelli Nova pump my cousin had loaned me was loaded with 3-inch shells containing buckshot.

"I knew I would have to act quickly to get a shot at the speed the 'buck' was slipping through the trees. I whistled sharply to see if I could get the deer to pause or slow, but to no avail. Swinging the barrel of the gun to the left, I placed the bead slightly in front of him and pulled the trigger, instantly pumping a second shell into the chamber. I missed completely!

"Then, a miracle! In the confusion of the loud explosion, the deer jumped, spun around from the direction he had been going, and provided me with a perfect profile in a clear lane through the brush. I put the bead on his shoulder and pulled the trigger again, hoping the larger shells would be enough to hit at that distance. The deer dropped suddenly and heavily, tumbling forward behind a large maple. One of the buckshot pellets hit the deer in the spine, and I could hear him struggling to stand, catching an occasional glimpse of antlers moving from behind the trunk.

"Afraid to try to climb down from my perch in the haze of adrenaline and lose sight of the deer if he moved, I waited until I heard the deer struggling less and less," Larry continued. "Then I lowered the gun carefully and climbed down, missing the last rung on the ladder in my excitement and painfully waiting to catch the wind that was knocked out of me.

"My cousin Arthur (I call him Art), who was up the nearby ridge and across two fields, finally turned his radio on. He had been tracking a doe when he heard me shoot and waited until he got the doe before turning his radio on. The first thing he did is ask me what I had shot.

"'I shot the biggest monster deer I've ever seen, Art.' I answered. I told him that I didn't want to get too close to the 'buck' in the brush in case it might still be alive and find the strength to jump and run. He told me to sit tight and that after he dragged his doe out of the woods he would work around behind me, and we could approach my deer together.

"When art arrived, we both eased into a line of sight with the deer, and he looked through the scope of his own shotgun and caught his breath. He couldn't believe the size. 'Larry, his rack is huge! And what mass,' Art said.

"When we finally got next to the massive body, we counted the points of the deer at least three or four times, as we kept losing count in our excitement. Thin, twisted tendrils of dried velvet still hung in the tines of the 15 beautiful points! The base of the antlers were easily four to five inches in circumference! Art picked me up off the ground in an excited bear hug. This one was bigger than the 10-point record buck he had taken just a few years earlier.

"Art was already thinking ahead. 'I've got to go get my camera before we dress him, and a trailer! This thing is huge!'

"After I marked and tied my tag to the right antler with a piece of string from my coat pocket, he asked me if I wanted to go with him to hook up the trailer. I told him no way. He left me sitting by the beautiful animal, trembling with excitement, stroking the still-warm flank of my trophy. When I finally heard him returning, I walked out to meet the vehicle and was surprised to see my Grandpa Ridley sitting in the passenger seat. Art had stopped to pick him up so he could see my buck.

"Grandpa, always the skeptic, after hearing how many points the deer had, counted them twice more, confirming what Art had already told him. A veteran hunter of over 45 years, Grandpa was impressed, and proud, of the deer, and me.

"As Art and I prepared to take some pictures, Grandpa lifted the buck's back leg and asked, 'What'd you do, already cut off his stuff?'

"Confused about the sudden turn of events, Art and I peered closer as I told him, 'No. Why would I? We wanted pictures first.'

"All three of us looked, finding nothing but the two rows of udders! None of us knew what to say as we stared dumbfounded into each other's faces.

"Then Art stated the obvious: 'It's a doe! A 15-point doe!' He and I never thought for a split second that the deer could have been anything but a buck when I tagged it.

"I was almost late for Thanksgiving dinner. I had something extra to be thankful for that year; a deer story to top them all! A 207 pound, field dressed, massively antlered 15-point doe! After having it officially scored, I discovered that my doe actually beats many record bucks. With a nontypical gross score of 181 3/8 and a net score of 165 2/8, my lovely lady with antlers entered me into the record books.

"For just a moment, I jokingly considered giving up hunting while I was ahead. Nah. I already love it too much!"

Realizing that many people might question that a deer with such a large set of antlers and body would be a doe, Larry took both still photos and video to verify the whitetail's sex. The whitetail obviously had hormonal problems to end up with such a large body and antlers. Due to the hormonal problems, the doe may not have been capable of producing fawns. The fact that she did not have any fawns with her and her exceptional body size are indications she had not given birth to fawns.

Many antlered does still have their antlers in velvet. An antlered doe with a 27-point nontypical rack, including drop tines from each beam, that was still covered in velvet was shot in Kansas on December 3, 2008 by Mike Smith from Clay Center. That rack had a gross score of 179, but the velvet covering of the antlers would have obviously inflated the score. Even with the velvet intact, that set of antlers did not score as high as the rack from the antlered doe Ridley shot.

There were still some dried pieces of velvet on the antlers of Larry's doe, indicating the velvet shedding was not normal in this case either. The doe was estimated to be 3 1/2 years old, based on tooth wear.

It's amazing the antlers from the antlered doe that Ridley shot scored as high as they did even though the beams were not very long and the inside spread was narrow. Tine length and mass played key roles in adding to the score.

The rack only had an inside spread of 13 6/8 inches. The right beam was 20 4/8 inches long and the left measured 22 1/8 inches. There were seven points on the right antler and eight on the left. Two of the tines on each antler were nontypicals and they had a total length of 12 6/8 inches.

The brow tines were much longer than normal, measuring seven and eight inches. The second and third tines on the right side were also long, taping 9 2/8 and 10 5/8 inches. The second tine on the left side was over 10 inches long (10 2/8), too, but the third tine was only 5 5/8 inches long.

The five inches difference in length between the third tines on each antler was one of the major deductions. There was an inch or more difference in most of the other tines, too. On top of that, the fifth typical tine on the left antler did not have a matching tine on the right side, resulting in a 1 7/8-inch deduction there. The total for deductions came to 16 1/8 inches.

The bases of the antlers were huge. The circumference of the right beam at the base was 6 7/8 inches and the left base measured 7 1/8 inches. The circumference on the right antler between the brow point and second tine was even larger at 9 3/8 inches, but the same measurement on the left antler was 5 5/8, resulting in a deduction of 3 6/8 inches for the difference.

Even with the large circumferences at certain places on the antlers, not all of those measurements were impressive. The smallest circumference was 3 7/8 inches. That was the fourth measurement on the right antler. The total of all eight circumference measurements came to 46 1/8 inches.

*Photo courtesy Alan Schultz*

*Alan Schultz with a monster 12-pointer scoring 177 7/8 that he saw the day before he got it. The buck was making huge rubs.*

# Chapter 15

# *Unreal Rubs*

Alan Schultz from Northville had been seeing some amazingly large antler rubs on his property for two years (2002 and 2003) without catching a glimpse of the deer that made them. Without seeing an antlered whitetail capable of making such sign and the fact that the rubs were so outlandishly large, Schultz started thinking they were fake.

"I actually thought one of my buddies was pulling a prank on me by making the rubs because the trees they were on were so big around and the rubbing was so high off the ground," Alan said.

The first large rub he found during 2002 was on a tree that was at least eight inches in diameter and it had been shredded. And the tree's bark was scarred much higher than normal. In late October of 2003, another spectacular rub appeared about 100 yards from the first one.

"That tree was 10 inches in diameter," Schultz said. "Again, the tree bark was shredded and, as I looked up at the remarkable height of the antler marks, I had a feeling of disbelief."

Alan's opinion about the rubs changed on the evening of November 28, 2003. He finally saw a buck he thought was capable of making them.

"When I drove home from work, he took off running through an apple orchard on our property," Schultz said. "I thought he was a 10-point with 10-inch tines."

That sighting was the key to Alan bagging the second highest scoring typical whitetail on record for Washtenaw County. It was a 12-pointer, not a 10, and the antlers had an impressive gross score of 183. After 5 1/8 inches of deductions were subtracted, the rack netted 177 7/8. The county's best typical is a 10-pointer netting 186 1/8 that Mark Ritchie shot on the second day of the 1984 gun season. The story about Ritchie's hunt for that buck is in Book 1 of Great Michigan Deer Tales.

The Schultz Buck was also the second highest scoring typical known taken in the state during 2003. Honors for the number one typical for the year went to Paul Calvert for a Jackson County 13-pointer that netted 178 4/8. Calvert got that buck with bow and arrow. The story behind Calvert's Boone and Crockett bow buck is included in another chapter in this book.

Until 2003, the best buck to Alan's credit was a 10-point that he got with bow and arrow a few years earlier. That rack scored between 128 and 130. The antlers from his Boone and Crockett buck in 2003 make the 10-point rack look small even though its larger than most hunters manage to shoot in Michigan. The comparison more accurately reflects how much larger than normal the 12-point is.

Schultz said he started deer hunting with bow and arrow when he was 13 years old and began hunting whitetails with firearms a year later when he turned 14. His first deer was a 6-point he got with a gun when he was 17. A year later, he got his first deer with bow and arrow, which was a doe. By 2003, he had been hunting whitetails for 32 years.

Never during those years of hunting, had he seen antler rubbed trees like those that began appearing on his property. He hasn't seen any rubs like that since then either.

"Two years ago (2002), I saw a rub that was unbelievable," Alan said when he was interviewed in 2004. "The tree it was on was huge, and it went way up the tree. The buck that made it came in one night and then disappeared. In October of 2003 I found another one of these big rubs no more than 100 yards from the other one."

The fact that the rubs were so much bigger and higher than any others he had ever seen combined with the failure of anyone who spent time on the property actually seeing a buck with antlers capable of making such sign, it was natural for Schultz to be puzzled by the rubs. He was so convinced they were fake that he hunted elsewhere during the first week of the 2003 gun season. He got a 10-pointer with a double brow tine on the right antler in Jackson County during the early part of the firearms hunt.

The rack from that buck was smaller than the antlers from his best bow kill, so he didn't bother having it measured.

The sighting of the big antlered buck on the evening of November 28 was literally an eye opener. Alan admits that if he hadn't seen the whitetail on the 28th, there's an excellent chance he would have hunted elsewhere on the 29th and may not have gotten one of Washtenaw County's best typicals.

"I told my wife and son about the buck and tried to get them to hunt for him with me the following evening," Schultz said. "My son couldn't make it, but my wife and I hunted. I was in a tree stand along a route that bucks often take when exiting the property. That's the way the buck went when I saw him the day before."

Alan added that the tree stand he occupied on the evening of November 29 was within 100 yards of their apple orchard and 125 yards from the large rub the buck had made that fall. The deer were active that evening. Schultz said he saw a 4-point buck, then a doe and a nice 8-pointer. After having seen the bigger whitetail, and the fact he had taken a 10-pointer in Jackson County, it was easy for him to pass up the 8.

The buck Alan was waiting for showed up about the same time he had been seen the day before; as light was fading for the day. He was about 100 yards away when Schultz first saw him and he was on the same trail the other deer had traveled.

"He moved extremely slowly," Alan wrote in an account of his hunt. "He would take one step, scan the area and then take another step. He was like a king coming down a stairway. One step, then a pause to look at his gallery. Another step, then a pause as if to say, 'Look at me. I am the man!'

"He was majestic and the fading autumn light gave him an even greater presence. He walked with the well deserved confidence of a buck that has survived many hunting seasons. He finally moved to within 80 yards. At this point, the anticipation, his pace and the fading light were almost hypnotizing.

**121**

"At the same time, it was driving me crazy. I decided that 80 yards and broadside was an acceptable shot. I brought my gun up ever so slowly and found him in the 3-9 power Bushnell scope. By then he had turned and was looking right at me, with his body angling toward me. I was really concerned.

"Had he seen me raise the gun even though my stand was high in the pines? Had his sixth sense told him I was there?

"I was confident in the gun, a 12 gauge Winchester pump. I had mounted the scope myself and sighted it in. The 2 3/4-inch Remington copper solid slugs I was shooting out of the rifled barrel were an inch high at 60 yards.

"I placed the crosshairs on his left shoulder, steadied myself and gently squeezed the trigger. The shot broke the silence and my hypnotic trance as it echoed through the cool air. The buck took off running like he had been shot out of a cannon. He ran low to the ground and disappeared after covering 25 yards.

"In the sudden acceleration of time," Alan continued, "I noticed two things of great importance. First, his tail was down. There was no white flag. Secondly, it looked like he was struggling on his left front leg, a clue my slug connected.

"I waited 10 minutes, slipped down from my stand and returned 45 minutes later with my Indian tracking squaw. That's what I call my wife, Eva, during deer season. She's the best tracker I know."

And Eva did find and follow the blood trail. With the aid of a flashlight, she found the dead deer about 100 yards from where Alan shot it.

"It was quite a surprise to walk up on this buck," Schultz commented. "When my wife found him she was hooting up a storm.

"I think the buck was moving around looking for a doe to be bred when I shot him," Alan stated. "None of the people hunting our property had seen him before. After I got him, a bowhunter told me he shot at the same deer four miles away."

After Schultz got the big buck, he called his cousin in Kalamazoo to ask him how to score the rack because he thought he had taken a Boone and Crockett deer. He was obviously right. He said he wasn't familiar with Commemorative Bucks of Michigan (CBM) and their big game scoring activities in the state until trying to get official measurements for the rack.

The buck was aged at 6 1/2. The carcass wasn't weighed, but Alan estimated its dressed weight at 200 pounds. The taxidermist thought it was heavier.

As Alan estimated when he first saw the booner, a number of the antler tines were close to 10 inches long and one of them exceeded that length. The third point on the left antler was 10 4/8 inches long. The second and fourth tines on that side were over nine inches in length. The third point on the right antler was 9 4/8 inches long and the fourth point was 1/8-inch shy of nine.

Both beams were over 26 inches long and the inside spread was 19 7/8 inches. A buck with that wide a rack would be able to rub big trees, which helps explain the size of the antler rubs Alan saw on his property. The circumferences at the base of both beams was five inches. There were no nontypical tines on the rack.

It should come as no surprise that it was a thrill for Schultz to bag a buck of that caliber. What may come as a surprise is he said he has seen a whitetail with a bigger rack. He saw the bigger deer in Jackson County a number of years earlier. His family nicknamed him Goliath.

"He might have been a world record," Alan commented. "He had 12 long points and the antlers were much wider than the one I got in 2003. The first time I saw him, I thought it was two deer standing next to one another, but it was just him. Then another deer walked out and Goliath dwarfed it."

Alan said he always saw Goliath at a distance; never close enough to get a shot at him. Schultz's brother eventually got a shot at that buck with bow and arrow, but failed to get it.

One of Alan's friends later shot the 8-pointer that Schultz passed up before shooting the booner. The smaller buck's rack had a 17 to 18-inch spread. Alan guessed that the antlers would have scored about 120.

Schultz got two more trophy bucks in Washtenaw County after 2003, both netting in the 150s, one of which was taken during the December muzzleloader season. In 2004 he got a nontypical 10-pointer that nets 150 4/8. Then in 2005, he got a book buck with 8 points that netted 151 1/8. Alan said he was on his way to hunt in

Jackson County that December morning during 2005 when his wife called his cell phone to tell him she just saw a big buck from their house.

When Schultz returned home later that day, he located the tracks of the big buck his wife had seen in the six to seven inches of snow that were on the ground. He said the whitetail had fed in an uncut cornfield and was heading toward a bedding area he was familiar with when his wife saw the deer. On the chance the buck might return to the same cornfield that evening, Alan posted 100 yards from the bedding area.

The whitetail appeared just before dark, walking in the same tracks it made going in the opposite direction during the morning. Those were the last tracks that deer made.

*Photo courtesy Alan Schultz*

*Alan Schultz displays the impressive antlers from the buck that was making the runreal rubs he saw.*

# *About the Author*

Richard P. Smith is an award winning outdoor writer and photographer living in Marquette, Michigan with his wife and business partner Lucy. He is a nationally recognized writer, photographer and speaker who has written 23 books and thousands of magazine articles. He is one of only four people in Michigan who have qualified for a Commemorative Bucks of Michigan (CBM) Grand Slam, which includes a deer, bear, elk and turkey that are all entered in state records maintained by CBM.

His best whitetail is a Saskatchewan 10-pointer he got in 1999 that qualified for honorable mention in Boone and Crockett Records with a net score of 163 7/8. Prior to that, he bagged a nontypical 12-pointer with a 9-inch drop tine from the same area that netted 165 3/8. His best Michigan buck is a typical 11-pointer he shot on public land in the Upper Peninsula (UP) that nets 148 4/8. He's taken a number of other bucks that score in the 140s.

A Saskatchewan black bear he bagged with a Knight muzzleloader during the spring of 2002 is the second highest scoring bruin in national muzzleloading records with a skull that measured 21 14/16. It's also in alltime Boone and Crockett Records. Since then, he collected two more trophy bruins with a muzzleloader that qualify for honorable mention in Boone and Crockett Records, with skulls scoring 20 2/16. Richard has four trophy bruins in Pope and Young Records that he got with bow and arrow and he also took a book bear with a muzzleloader in Michigan.

One of Smith's latest books, Black Bear Hunting, was published by Stackpole Books during 2007. Stackpole also published several of the author's other popular books, including the 3rd edition of Deer Hunting and Stand Hunting For Whitetails.

Smith is a Field Editor for Bear Hunting Magazine and Michigan Hooks & Bullets. He's the editor for Bear Facts, a quarterly newsletter published by the Michigan Bear Hunters Association. He writes for Woods-N-Water News, Michigan Outdoor News, Michigan Sportsman Magazine and the Porcupine Press on a regular basis. His writing and photography have been published in national magazines including Deer & Deer Hunting, North American Whitetail, Buckmasters, Outdoor Life, American Hunter, Bowhunter and National Wildlife.

The author is a recognized expert on whitetail deer and black bear behavior and biology as well as hunting these species of big game.

# Books by Richard P. Smith

Regardless of where you hunt whitetails, the inspirational stories in this set of books can help you learn how to be a better hunter! If you are interested in bagging a BOOK BUCK, studying this collection of success stories will help make it happen. Each book contains a different set of short stories to entertain and educate you. **Save $ on Sets!**

**Deer Tales Book Sets - 2 for $28; 3 for $40; 4 for $50; 5 for $60**

**Great Michigan Deer Tales, Book 5** - NEW - Short stories from every region of the state about 28 more monster bucks taken by Michigan men and women with centerfire guns, muzzleloaders and bow and arrow, including some of state record proportions, that are sure to entertain, inspire and surprise you. (128 pages; 32 photos)
**Price: $16.50 postpaid**

**Great Michigan Deer Tales, Book 4** - Whopper whitetails bagged in each region of the state are covered. Every chapter has at least one important lesson and some of them are loaded with important information for hunters. Read new information about the Rompola Buck, including a photo of the huge typical when it was alive. Find out about a World Record 8-Point bagged in Michigan. (128 pages; 38 photos)
**Price: $16.50 postpaid**

**Great Michigan Deer Tales, Book 3** - Two chapters are devoted to unraveling the mystery behind a 12-pointer scoring more than the current world record that Mitch Rompola shot with bow and arrow during 1998. Other chapters are devoted to outstanding hunts shared by men, women and youngsters, including one of the state's most successful senior citizens and much, much more. (128 pages; 47 photos)
**Price: $16.50 postpaid**

**Great Michigan Deer Tales, Book 2** - More Great Deer Tales. Read about the current state record typical taken in Jackson County during 1996. Find out about the biggest bucks bagged by women in the state. Learn about trophy bucks with locked antlers. Read about a trophy rack recovered after almost 40 years and the end of a 70-year mystery surrounding a B&C nontypical. (128 pages; 46 photos)
**Price: $16.50 postpaid**

**Great Michigan Deer Tales, Book 1** - Learn How, Where and When some of the state's Biggest Bucks were bagged, including a Boone & Crockett bow kill taken in 1985 by Mitch Rompola from Traverse City. Read about whitetails with the largest ANTLERS as well as those that were the HEAVIEST and OLDEST. (128 pages; 40 photos)
**Price: $15.50 postpaid**

**Tracking Wounded Deer - 2nd Edition** - Learn how to recover all of the deer you shoot. Decide when to begin tracking, determine type of hit and distinguish between tracks of wounded and healthy deer. This book is must reading for bowhunters since trailing arrowed deer is part of every successful hunt. Eight pages of color photos show blood and hair sign. (160 pages; 72 photos) **Price: $19.50 postpaid**

**Stand Hunting for Whitetails (Revised)** - Detailed coverage of the tricks of the trade for hunting from ground-based stands as well as tree stands with gun and bow. Read about Boone and Crockett bucks and a hunt with baseball great Wade Boggs. Stand hunting is the most popular and effective whitetail hunting method. Learn how to do it more effectively! (256 pages; 181 photos) **Price: $18.50 postpaid**

**Deer Hunting - 3rd Edition** - This best selling book was so popular it was updated in 2003 to include even more information and photographs, making it one of the most comprehensive books in print on the subject. Learn all you need to know to successfully hunt whitetails and mule deer. There are bonus chapters on deer diseases and management, hunting ethics and more. For beginners or experienced veterans like the author. (325 pages; 139 photos) **Price: $23.00 postpaid**

**Animal Tracks & Signs Of North America** - It's the first guide book including actual photos of wildlife tracks and sign rather than sketches. Bonus chapters cover aging tracks, tracking wildlife and much more. (271 pages; 200 photos) **Price: $23 postpaid.**

**Understanding Michigan Black Bear - 2nd Edition** - Learn all about black bears; their habits, life history, behavior and how to avoid problems from them when in bear country. One of the chapters is a history of bear attacks. The text provides valuable insights into bear research and management. (256 pages; 126 photos) **Price: $19.50 postpaid**

**Black Bear Hunting** – This hard cover book is the **BEST** ever written about black bear hunting. All aspects of bear hunting are covered: baiting, dogging, spotting and stalking, calling, hunting natural food sources, field judging bears, shot placement, trailing wounded bears and much, much more. The chapter on field judging black bears alone is worth the cost of this book. So is information about how to score on bruins that only visit baits after dark. (384 pages; 200+ color photos) **Price: $38.00 postpaid**

# www.RichardPSmith.com

# Book Order Form

**Quantity**                                                                 **Price**

_____ **Great Michigan Deer Tales-Book 5 ($16.50)**          _____

_____ **Great Michigan Deer Tales-Book 4 ($16.50)**          _____

_____ **Great Michigan Deer Tales-Book 3 ($16.50)**          _____

_____ **Great Michigan Deer Tales-Book 2 ($16.50)**          _____

_____ **Great Michigan Deer Tales-Book 1 ($15.50)**          _____

_____ **Deer Tales Sets -**
    **2 for $28; 3 for $40; 4 for $50; 5 for $60**          _____
    **Please specify which books sent to the same address.**
    **Save $21.50 on the complete set.**

_____ **Tracking Wounded Deer ($19.50)**                        _____

_____ **Stand Hunting for Whitetails ($18.50)**                 _____

_____ **Deer Hunting - 3rd Edition ($23)**                          _____

_____ **Animal Tracks & Signs of N.A. ($23)**                    _____

_____ **Understanding Michigan Black Bear ($19.50)**        _____

_____ **Black Bear Hunting ($38.00)**                               _____

Total Payment Enclosed          $ _____

**Name**_____

**Address** _____

**City** _____ **State** _____ **Zip** _____

**Please remit by MasterCard, Visa, check or money order.**
**Circle card type:**
**MC/Visa#** _____

**Expiration Date** _____ **Signature** _____
**Phone#** _____

**Please send US funds. Canadian orders add $3/book.**
Prices include postage and handling. Make checks payable to:

## Smith Publications
814 Clark Street,
Marquette, MI 49855
## www.RichardPSmith.com